Afghanistan and Iraq

Seth Lombardy

This book is dedicated to the men and women assigned to Bravo Company, 1st Battalion, 87th Infantry of the 10th Mountain Division (Light Infantry) during Operation Enduring Freedom IV (Afghanistan, July 2003 to April 2004) and Echo Troop, 2nd Squadron of the 11th Armored Cavalry Regiment during Operation Iraqi Freedom III (Iraq, January 2005 to December 2005)

Table of Contents

Afghanistan and Iraq

Seth Lombardy

ISBN (Print Edition): 978-1-09832-522-0

ISBN (eBook Edition): 978-1-09832-523-7

Afghanistan

There is nothing apparent there. It is so desolate and unforgiving on contact that you seem to know immediately that there will never be anything there that you and I as Westerners will ever understand or cling to with affection. The Graveyard of Empires is appropriately named. 9/11 is one of the most shocking and effective attacks in the history of warfare. Its impact is still undefined. Though there is much debate on whether wars in these regions are fought for freedom or oil; though the Soviets had had their version of our Vietnam War end here only a decade prior; though there is ample documentation going back to Alexander of reasons why Afghanistan should not be occupied, here I was standing at the back of a C-5 Galaxy in the middle of the night in Kandahar as the back door opened and the summer heat came roiling in to greet us in the middle of July 2003.

So, we're off the plane and filing off the tarmac. We start finding our tents and scurrying through the dark, dusty streets of our new home looking for phones and computers to let our loved ones know that we were here. Just a few hours before I had watched North Africa pass beneath our aircraft as the sun was setting and thinking to myself that the next place I would see in daylight would be Afghanistan. We had left Fort Drum in Upstate New York almost a day before and now here we were. Seamless transition. Very touristy except for the fact that you are reminded you are an infantryman in an infantry unit every five to seven seconds and that the root word of infantry is infant. It's just the way it is: Absurd but necessary, but constantly vexatious to a semi-intelligent mind. You don't have to be very smart to understand the need for everyone to hem in everyone in a place that has the potential to wipe you away like the endless dust and snow that have passed through here through the ages. You really don't want to die there and if you've ever read of war in Afghanistan's history, you don't want to die at the hands of the people who live there. So, stick together children. Watch each other and constantly keep at least one kid in the nursery crying.

We settle into our tent and the disposable cameras come out in the age before social media - and what is the beginning of the end of commercial analog photography. Different groupings based on teams and squads, then affiliations and weaponry, and pre-smart-phone selfies that required several weeks before finding out whether you successfully pulled off the arm's-length vanity pose. We had to develop film still. Then, you have to figure out what time it is and set watches and understand Greenwich Mean Time (GMT) and that though we were in the dark of night, we were on London time (Basically – London is GMT + 1) and that was how everyone synchronized from the little guy to the big guy. Then sleep. A brief sleep. Lots of little brief sleeps.

Physical fitness and battle drills and weapon-zeroing and leisurely strolls by the burning trash pits. Guard in varying forms to break up sleep even more. After about a week in country we hopped on a bird for Bagram Air Base which is north of Kandahar in Kabul where we would assume a full interior guard posture as part of the air base's defense. This simply means: You, - grab your buddy and go sit in this wooden box on the perimeter and look for anything ....bad. This is the wait part of hurry-up-and wait. It's every desert poet's premise:

The horizon, the perimeter, the edge of civilization, the unknown just ahead, the fragile existence in the remnants that are your life - on hold, for the unseen that awaits you. Time stands still but you still get tired.

It's here in these towers that you run across new ways to combine doing your duty with entertainment. It is also where you get to discover the commerce of your companions. I got this great pen from my fellow tower guard: the F-301. It is a superb writing tool for when you have sweaty hands and dripping brow and you want to avoid smearing or smudging. With this fine instrument and some waterproof paper, I started sketching my range card. Weapons dynamics, positions of terrain features, orientation of the compass, etc.

On the northwest corner of Bagram Airfield there were these very nice houses (by comparison with their neighbors in other sectors) and gardens. It was the gardens that diffused the imagery of the houses and made them look better than they probably were. Very green, and it greatly contrasted the grey-brown smudge of everything else. Drawing range cards allowed me to simultaneously stay focused, be productive, and achieve my first in-depth perspective of the world outside of the wire. During these guard shifts, Mars was the closest it had been in a while, so there was something to search for in the night sky. During the day, if you got a tower at the long end of the runway you got the entertainment of A-10s soaring over your roof on their way to close-air support missions, or the occasional F-15 that would remove your soul and set it next to you for a moment. The sheer power of that aircraft is unbelievable.

Jay-Z's The Black Album had dropped and on one shift I was with a dude who sang the songs almost non-stop. On another post, one of the platoons in our company had committed some infraction or indiscipline and spent almost my whole post (their whole sleep time) standing guard - posted tactically across the Hesco walls, facing outboard. Basically, they did my job for me which is nice. Then there was one last post where I had my first bout with a stomach bug. Whether it was the Malaria medication, the food, lack of hydration, or what have you- it was immediate and vicious. I passed out in the porta-john only to be revived by its essence. With a very irritated bootyhole from wiping too much - thinking I was good to go about fifty times - I managed to get back up to my post and that was all she wrote. Guard came to an end. It was finally time to move out into the Graveyard of Empires and do our part to keep ourselves (and our empire) from meeting the myriad of fates that await foreigners in Bactria (the ancient term for Afghanistan).

We took Chinooks to Orgun-E Kalan which is located at the north end of the Bermel Valley along the eastern edge of the country. You don't journey anywhere farther than twenty or thirty miles without a helicopter or a fixed-wing aircraft. I do remember the first thing we did and that was occupy a gutted building. This would be where our platoon would house itself for a bit. Moving out of here were some French commandos. Maybe Foreign Legion. I don't know. One particular salty old Frenchman let me take his picture, so maybe not. He was a stoic-looking fellow and he had a Hemingway like nature to him. If nothing, a Hemingway character. Khakis, button down dress shirt, boots. These men were definitely working outside of the scope of conventional forces and this our role in many respects: To hold down the forts for special operations forces. This is not to say that we weren't there to do the same or saying that we did not execute like-missions, because we did- as I will light upon in Iraq. But, the war in Afghanistan

- and the Global War on Terror in general - is not and never has been a conventional fight. This is about hunting game, not testing rank and file against other chessmen from a formal body-politic. This is game hunting, specifically.

There was a large sign specifying the presence of an ODA, or Operational Detachment – Alpha: A U.S. Special Forces A-Team. Also not an anomaly and very much the standard and not the exception as to what was right about this fight. There were old cobbled buildings and immediately there was the mess hall and the only two-story structure on the camp. Next to this building was a small patch of large sunflowers. At the base of the sunflowers were kittens that were recently born and played there in the evenings when we were in line to eat.

I have three memories of eating chow here: One was strolling my happily-fed self out of the building and throwing my tray in the garbage and walking off back to my tent, only to realize later that I had used my $60 Gerber tool to cut my steak and lobster (don't ask) and with no regard, as if to say- "whatever", it went with the paper tray and the remnants of the meal into the garbage. Some Afghani would have it by nightfall. You're welcome, whomever. I know you appreciated it. I bet that Gerber is still in the Bermel Valley. Second, I was doing that ever leisurely Lombardy stroll. I turned a corner to a violent blast that did the same thing as that F-15 and dislodged my soul from my body. I had walked straight towards the front range fan of a 105mm artillery piece that had made its position inside the camp along the path between the mess hall and the birthing areas. The other was eating chow with a kid who would be dead in a matter of days. Nice guy, no pretenses. He was in another company and I had no familiarity or bond beyond that meal. He would die in a wadi, outside of a place called Shkin- which was at the south of the Bermel Valley and where my tale of Afghanistan essentially ends in operational terms several months from this point. A wadi, for which much of these tales occur- are the prevalent feature on these valley floors. Ever seen a healthy brain and the intersped patterns of worming matter? The draws inbetween are wadis. Lowland draws that easily break up flatland and make normal cohesion of groups travelling through very difficult. Fireteams which are the basic maneuver unit of an Infantry squad and are usually composed of a team leader and three Soldiers, can easily be separated in terms of line-of-sight while patrolling wadis due to maintaining sensible ballistic distance between each other (Hand grenade range usually). I do not know his full story. Only that he was cut off and bled out and died during a 12-hour battle that included the Taliban going after Medevac choppers. His body was transported north to our camp before heading back to one of the hubs (Bagram or Kandahar) and then back to the United States for burial. The last I saw of my noble dinner guest was his field ambulance leaving the camp to be helicoptered out of the valley. We lined the dirt road leading to the landing zone and saluted as he passed by. His body was loaded in a dignified manner by a casket team at the half-step, up the ramp of the bird, and then gone to the sky.

The time came to make our first patrol out of the camp. Kind of a warm-up if you will. It was late afternoon. Overcast, which was nice. Warm, but not hot, which was also nice. It was a simple patrol for which I have no recollection of purpose. I remember some racket or what not (maybe gunfire) and we all took a knee. Maybe that was the reason. Random gunfire at a wedding, maybe; something. I was on point. Our company first sergeant was patrolling with us, as was very common here at 10th Mountain. Very professional and very dedicated leadership. Ramped up and assholes at times, but hey- whatever. The tradeoff for that sincerity was worth the occasional reaming as an individual or group. He knelt behind me and asked plainly what was up? He had a friendly air and that made it easier to just communicate, "I don't know, First Sergeant". Pretty much the only time that answer is reasonable. Nothing came of this and we walked back. Our platoon sergeant mentioned the lines of rock that were intermittent on the trail and to be cognizant of possible explosive ordinance. Check and check.

There was an artillery and/or rocket attack during this time and it may have occurred while in the chow hall, but for some reason I don't remember much about it. Many more would follow, and they are always fascinating moments. YouTube has Orgun and many of the places I talk about here.

Physical fitness training continues just as it was when in garrison. Physical fitness is king in the Army and especially the Infantry and for a good damn reason. I won't bore you too much with the physical requirements of combat, but they are extensive. Add in environmental factors like this valley floor we were on being at 6800' above sea level and the median daytime temperature being at 120°F, and extremely dry. This contrasts greatly with the summer temperature of Fort Drum being around 80 or 90°F, humid, and only about 300 feet above sea level. You not only have to acclimate on the basic physiological level, but you have to rework your professional regimen and adapt your fighting abilities to your new ecosystem. How does this fit into patrolling and guard cycles? Well, essentially you lose sleep. You have to take time to exercise where you would normally have free time. You lose sleep to a lot of things in combat and I like sleep. No, I love sleep. That being said, you're not alone in this like-love relationship. Like the rest of the hardships, you are not alone and that makes it easier to deal with.

It was during the physical fitness hours of the morning that the next series of happenings occurred that stand the test of time (17 years as of the authoring of this). All three have to do with my platoon sergeant. The first is relative to the sleep aspect. Very brief and rare to be sure, I saw my platoon leader and platoon sergeant having an argument over sleep. I don't remember who was pro-sleep and who was pro-fuckthoseguys, but I think the platoon leader was all about getting an extra wink while our platoon sergeant, a daunting and fierce man, was all about dragging dicks through the morning dust. Like I mentioned, it was brief. Both were very professional leaders and knew better than to let that window of shared dialogue get away from them.

The next incident was a culminating point in the adjusting period. Mind you, we had been in country for less than two months. You don't just transition into this life of combat overnight. All of this acclimation is both physical and mental and requires a lot of grinding gears; personalities come apart and get put back together a few times before everything starts to make sense and life becomes, "normal." Don't ever think that units just whoosh in to stay with ease. In a foreign land for a long duration that entails the myriad tasks required to sustain fighting ability, units don't have their shit together day one or day sixty. If you are there to live and fight, you live and fight just as you do anywhere else: Through trial and error and character. We all formed up to go run outside the wire in a clearing that had the general shape of a long ancient athletic track and field. Just think worn path in circular form and rocks. That's it. Maybe it didn't need all those poetics.

Before we got special shotguns that attached to our rifles beneath the barrels, team leaders (which I was one) had to carry shotguns to breach locks on doors and possibly use for close-quarters in a house. Our service rifles, M-4 carbines, were very sleek in base unit form, and very light. But, have it as you will- things start piling up and getting attached to it: Lasers, optics, grenade launchers, pressure switches for each; you name it. Kitchen sink stuff. On this morning, I decided, "You know what, Sergeant Lombardy- fuck this rifle and running with it. Grab that shotgun and take it light, Brother."

I knew that that shotgun was of no use out there in the wide open, but my economic mind worked out a quick approximation of: If shit goes down out there in a direct-engagement (that's eyeball to eyeball with the enemy), it would be weirder than weird because it's super wide out there: Vast flat valley floor. The Bermel Valley has more than twenty or so miles of range between two sets of mountains. Maybe less. More than a few football fields for sure. There are tower guards. There's a lot of activity moving about in vehicles. Let's just say, if for some reason- the Taliban decided to do an assault across the plain- it would be so ludicrous that I couldn't even insult the Taliban with this scenario. Not that they hadn't - and not that they wouldn't; because - if they want to fight, they will take you to task no matter what you have with you or what stands against them: Natural, mechanical, or otherwise. If some cleric convinced them to run across the Bermel Valley, they would. Fierce. However, not today. I was sure of it. Haha. So, with no further adieu: Shotgun in hand, I strolled out to formation.

Platoon sergeants have shitty days. They really do. They have a lot to worry about and there's only so much one can take in each of these 24-hour periods before they lose their collective shit and have to educate you and your platoon-mates. Sometimes, this anger and frustration accumulates even before the day really begins. Whatever got under my platoon sergeant's skin that morning is beyond me, but I just happened to get a little bit of that free chicken. I knew he would notice the shotgun and lo-and-behold he did. Something about, "Buck Sergeant" started the one-way conversation off followed by an unnecessary but very platoon-sergeantish education on weapons capabilities and my obvious poor choice. He finished with, "You have a screw loose." In the back of my head I was like, "That's because I'm hanging out here with a loose nut." Believe you me, that shit didn't leave my lips. He then went on tearing up my squad leader before finishing his morning breakfast of 30 assholes.

Then. Then there was Shoes and Biscuits. Shoes and Biscuits didn't get his name from me until later in the game, but Shoes and Biscuits makes his intro here to finish off the PT story triptych. Shoes and Biscuits and I didn't get along. This was a natural conflict. He didn't respect me, or anyone for that matter- but this wasn't uncommon amongst Soldiers and their leaders. Not to say this doesn't grow, but in this case- our personalities were either so much alike or so far apart as to be irreconcilable. Pick one. One day my platoon sergeant came strolling up to my tower with a big shit eating grin. I was, on one hand, pleasantly surprised to see him smiling but was quickly removed from this comfort when he let me know that he found Shoes and Biscuits playing a handheld electronic game in one of the other towers. What I am getting at here is, neither of these two could be trusted if they either (a) were smiling towards me and/or (b) trying to be friendly with me. This (b) part with Shoes and Biscuits came one morning after PT. We had done our thing; many of us had conducted hygiene and showered and even ate chow. The general air was at ease as if to say: We had arrived. Well. Shoes and Biscuits comes racing up to me and his manner is much less abrasive and non-condescending and very "Hey Buddy uhm I mean… Sergeant…uuuuh." After the Uh part, came, "Sergeant I left my weapon in the shower."

The sun dropped out of the sky and all was dark and cloudy. No wait, a blackhole opened up and the void wrote a check. No, no- that's still not a good enough description. This is a dark, sticky, horrible feeling that descended. Not only is losing your rifle a cardinal sin, where we were inside this camp with the Taliban in disguise essentially cleaning our showers, doing our laundry, and rummaging through our daily business as laborers- this was suddenly a very deadly possibility of that weapon of ours being turned on us: Nothing like the thought of handing your enemy your rifle and saying, "Shoot me and/or my buddies." Everyone is obviously locked-and-loaded out here and if such a thing did happen, it would be short-lived. But a life is super precious. I can't begin to express to you how real this becomes: A human being is irreplaceable in the fabric of the communities they come to inherit. They can be substituted, but they can no longer complement the rest as they did when they were alive. To have a guy you don't know die because you left a weapon laying around, is beyond any excuse, leaving too many unanswered questions. Once it is discovered it becomes the pivot and the singularity for the hell that follows for this trespass.

I was Shoes and Biscuit's team leader. Besides punishment for him, this should by any means- at least get me in trouble, too; and- quite possibly relieved for cause. Something odd happened in this moment. As we were all (the squad as a whole) gathered before our platoon sergeant inside our building, the long didactic narrative began with the directed-worthy-anger doled out with the inflection of our platoon sergeant's voice as he explained how he was having a great day until some smirky asshole from another unit mentioned the rifle in the chow hall to a collective leadership eating their breakfast and that he had confidently dismissed it as, "Not my guys!"; only to be corrected, "It belongs to one of your guys." As he individually started tearing up Shoes and Biscuits he passed right over me and went to our squad leader, with two things, "If something like this ever happens again, I will forget about all of the good things you have done." The squad would have to lay out weapons and ammo every hour on the hour for a week. Remember that sleep stuff? Yeah, anyways.

Not just lay out our drums and magazines, either. We had to shuck all of the rounds out of the magazines and line them up in addition to yanking the linked ammo to the SAWs out of their drums and "nutsacks" (small, thickly-woven nylon pouches that secure 100-round links), taking all of the 40mm rounds for M203 grenade launcher out of the grenadier vests that had poorly made brass-snap buttons; all of our pyro, all of our grenades, claymores, and Lord only knows what else we had? Oh yeah, AT4s I think. One or two of those. By the time you do this, it's time to do it again. Maybe it was every two hours? Regardless, man, what a pain in the ass. Our platoon sergeant put his cot next to ours as if to babysit his wayward children and I would look over his shoulder as he was watching Mash episodes and stewed over this set-back. Mind you, this all reasonable, really. I held no grudge on it then, and I certainly never considered retracting it in the future. To get to my point on the strange occurrence: He never said anything to me about it. He didn't mention it then, or ever to me. I was shocked. I took it as a gift. Honestly, I tried everything to be Shoes and Biscuits friend, on top of being his team leader. After about three or four days our platoon sergeant cut us loose from the corrective training. After this, our squad leader was a bit different. Not bad, but he definitely leaned a little harder.

Our second trip out of the wire was longer and involved staying out overnight. Another milestone. I don't remember this specific task and purpose of the extended patrol, but it was inclusive with the generality of looking for OBL (implied task), gathering intelligence (reporting takes care of this as a tool for aggregating intelligence), engaging the local populace in a dignified posture (diplomacy), and engaging hostile enemy forces if and when you make contact. This was a company sized mission with two platoons patrolling and a third platoon (second platoon to be specific) serving as transportation. The second platoon would man Humvees with crew-served weapons mounted on them (.50 cals and Mk-19 Grenade Launchers – a belt-fed machine gun for 40mm grenades); and, serve as the drop-off/pick-up vehicles and perform LOGPACs (or, logistics packages) for resupply. Very efficient task-organization.

We rolled out of the firebase at Orgun and drove into the foothills to the east. This is really the first time we were on our own beyond the protective enclave of an outpost. If something happened, it would be as-is- with no immediate chance to duck back to the wire. Here we were, nothing "training" about it and big-boy pants and big-boy (this part reads: Heavy) rucksacks on our backs. Summer day in Afghanistan and overcast. The overcast is really a blessing and I cannot stress it enough. It not only reduces the radiating heat of direct sunlight but makes the act of seeing a much easier thing. It is extremely bright in the desert and often compares to the effects of snow in daylight. From snow blindness in winter at Fort Drum to the desert equivalent. We arrived at our drop-off point at the base of a hill: The colors were yellowish terrain with the usual minimal brush, grey sky, green trucks and gear, raccoon eyes everywhere (sunglasses still important), and tan uniforms holding up the green splotches of ruck and kit seemingly suspended at a glance in midair by the effects of camouflage.

The first couple of hundred meters in Afghanistan were of course, uphill. I'm sure you've heard your fair share of descriptors of "searing-pain" in the legs from such activity, so I'll spare you that. I was really fit. Very fit. But it still hurt. I turned around at the top of the hill, feeling that pain but not bothered- too much - to find my SAW gunner struggling to the point of giving up and carelessly tossing his weapon down ahead of him as if it was a mountaineer's axe. I walked back down to the point where he was and chiding him simply with: "Dude we are just getting started." It came out a little harsher than that, but even my 'harsh' is well-groomed and dignified. He caught his wind and we carried on.

The sun came out and we stayed on the high ground. Squads spread out and the sister first platoon was somewhere a few hilltops over. Everywhere is uphill and disconnected inbetween. You might see someone next door but the effort to get there was an excruciating parabolic function. Memory fades here as to the context and particulars except for a few other images and poetics:

It came time for water re-supply, which meant finding a point on the map where second platoon would either meet us with the water or leave it cached for pick-up. Once we moved to the re-supply point we would have to gather it and carry it back to the patrol base or wherever the platoon was halted, depending on the tactical situation. Water is heavy. Seven pounds per gallon or something like that. The platoon leader called on our squad for the mission and we merrily set-out. The re-supply had had to move on for whatever reason, but they did the neatest thing that was a hat-tip to the endless tales of ingenuity in warfare: They had found a wadi with a small stream and a place where the water pooled and was hedged by a large stone. They left the water in the water and sent a grid location to the platoon leader. When we got there, there they were: thirty or forty bottles of water bobbing around or rested against shore and stone. Simple, efficient, and conforming to the land and situation.

We conducted movement through the night, looking for an ambush site if I remember correctly. Sometime before dawn we finally set up on a hilltop and kind of just sat there in physiological twilight. I like my sleep. Pretty sure I mentioned that already, and my eyes were heavy, and my neck was loose. Daylight popped up like a cartoon and with no enemy to speak of we moved to an extraction point where we would get picked up and taken back to Orgun. Once we got on the vehicles you could look around and see how tired everyone was.

Driving back we ran across camels and their herders. Camels are nasty and not to be messed with, but what a fantastic thing to be out in the world where such beasts run free and are a natural occurrence. Pulling into Orgun, the Special Forces A-Team that I mentioned earlier were getting ready to leave and their persons, vehicles, and equipment were a sight to see; but- so was the prospect of getting rested-up. That always buzzkills any marvel, real or perceived.

One evening, walking around - I came upon the backside of our building to the oddest sight: A group of Afghanis had gathered to commune, as was common. Their full attention was on a man who had showed up in full flowery man-dress, make-up, beads, and a boombox. He swirled and danced and turned like an ancient belly dancer. Our platoon leader had briefed us before leaving Drum that, "Women were for children; men were for pleasure." I had read some of the accounts of the Special Forces teams that opened up Afghanistan in the months after 9/11 and the reports of the "Girly Boys", but none of this had been seen until now. I stood and watched for a good five minutes. Here was military intelligence and old-world tales manifesting into fact. This was Afghanistan in one of its forms, and it was to be acknowledged and respected at a distance.

Morning physical training came and went on August 31st, 2003. For some reason I remember the platoon being very jovial and joking as we prepared to do whatever there was to do. In hindsight I wonder if it is a defense mechanism of sort but – no, we were doing okay. The large room and its rows of cots and its thirty odd infantrymen suddenly zeroed in on the radio operator's kit which was receiving traffic and could be heard due to the speaker that was used during times when radio monitoring could be open and non-tactical. The transmission was between a tactical controller and a helicopter crew and the information being exchanged was a nine-line medevac report. Everyone was now drawn to the electronic voices that were originating in the southern end of our valley in the vicinity of Shkin. The platoon huddle around the radio became dense in the effort to decipher who, what, where, when, how, etc?

Whatever really happened on that hill, I do not know. One of the men killed was one of my former Soldiers before deployment. He was a funny guy and even though he was the source of a bit of agony, I truly liked him as a person. He was all heart. Before deployment he got drunk one night and was talking shit to a senior Specialist we called Big Al. Big Al is a first sergeant as of the writing of this memoir. However Big Al wasn't about to get his hands dirty so he went and told First Sergeant who was a consummate professional and always working. First Sergeant told Big Al to send the mighty warrior his way for some quick counsel in hopes of steering a bad incident from being worse. No man likes to be told what to do. Big Al came back,

"First Sergeant wants to see you."

"You tell First Sergeant to come see ME!"

Well it didn't take long for First Sergeant to get down that hallway, kick his door open, and ask him loudly,

"Who the fuck do you think you are?!"

I don't remember what Adam's response was, but he lost his rank.

I am friends with his mother and check in on her from time to time and August 31st of each year in particular. I personally honor brazen actions near and far that have no real malice. Adam was funny, had a big heart, smiled all of the time, and used to loudly mock his old platoon sergeant who was a Samoan that used to heartily warn his troops he was angry with a loud, "OOOOOOOH MMMMAAAAAN."

Our battalion commander spoke to us before a memorial service scheduled to close the evening of August 31st, 2003. You get good things from battalion commanders when they speak. It is one of those stratas of leadership that when the layers are permeated, the relational system of command and unit take on a more congenial feel for a moment. It is one of their few practical chances to actually address their units as wholes because of the operational tempo and the fact that there are several layers of active training and leadership being executed beneath them that can't be effective with too much undue influence of rank. What I took from this one was a simple and sensible parable, "remember that most of these people are guilty of nothing except being poor." I really liked that and that stuck in my own development of ideas and ethos. I knew what it was like to be poor. The art of counseling in the military is a wide range of tools, from the physical to the passive. This was a commander's way of employing one of his own: Empathy. Have empathy. Start there or whatever else follows will all be lost. Conduct yourselves with this in mind.

Khost. Chinooks landed in a large cobble airfield. Wet. It had rained. It was green. Very contrasted to the inner portion of Afghanistan. Close to Pakistan is what the terrain change means. Or, any of the other former Soviet Republics for that matter. The Italians were here. Khost wasn't nearly as developed as it was when the suicide bomber attacked the CIA compound a few years later. There was an airstrip and a camp with large green tents enclosed by three foot high sandbag walls and make-shift porches. The first thing I ran into was the Italian meals. These things were fantastic. Big OD green bags with a coloration that was distinctly not of the American palette, but fascinatingly European. You are "poor" in war. You usually end up in war as a consequence of being poor. This is what poor people do: They window shop and marvel at simple sundries. Tactile microeconomics of the Soldier is the tactile microeconomics of the Poor. A perfect mirror.

And of course, we go straight into guard. Twelve hours on and twelve hours "off". Poor people work hard, long hours, led by professionals who work even harder. I am complaining. Everyone complains about this. Up and down the line; up and down the command structure. Never-ending. Better known as force protection, guard is the test of everything in one's own constitution because it is so monotonous that to describe it is to describe nothing. I guess that is what you can attribute to the running of a professional army or the administration of a government infrastructure: If you do it well enough, nothing is apparent; even to the participants. Well, the obvious first, last, and always requirement of security makes guard a very apparent necessity.

I had night shift. There were two of us at Sherman Gate to start off with. Twelve hours is a long time. You start cycling through the regime of snacking, chatting, doing radio checks, making or checking range cards, reporting information (which there was never any), ripping into whatever tobacco products you have, and then eventually everything turns into a talent show. My contribution to the stage of the eternal characters of military reminisce and parody was my uncanny and impeccable one-man act of doing every character in the jail cell scene from the movie Trading Places.

On occasion we would switch up and down the channels and find other towers so we could have a brief dialogue. No cell phones or smart phones. They really didn't exist yet in the way that they are now. They were a luxury. You had to be careful not to jump on a net that was monitored by command. However, we got coordinated enough to run a brief radio show that we called Misery Loves Company.

Beyond that, there was nothing notable about guard. First, last, always.

Patrols led to farms and towns. Kneeling in a field one day, I looked to my right and I'll be damned if there wasn't a midget Afghan farmer with an AK-47 strapped to his person, throwing him off balance with each step. There were lots of other rifles that assessed him before he got to me. I don't remember his circumstance, just him. A midget farmer with a Kalashnikov. And that definitive Russian object brings to memory recent history again: Outside of Khost were numerous ghosts of the Soviet Army: Abandoned artillery pieces and strangely crafted patrol bases formed like naturally-pulped wasp nests. Leafy trees. Eucalyptus. There was nothing here, either, though, really.

November arrived. November was a leap. Something broke the paradox of Achilles not being able to overtake the tortoise. One day, we got on C-130s on the airstrip at Khost to go to Bagram for a Joint Task-Force mission of some form or another. Aircraft had to make short take-offs and landings at Khost. For takeoff, this meant going full throttle and then nearly vertical. The runway is short because it is built on a plateau. You have to ramp up full throttle so as not to fall off the end and into a wadi-turned-chasm. There is an equally terrifying reason and that is to counter potential Taliban with surface to air missiles or the urge to execute random marksmanship training with a rifle. Many aviators and planes and their cargoes have gone down to a farmer with a rifle. Engines at a roar, brakes release, swing to the side from the acceleration, nose up; way up. Weightlessness. So that's what that feels like. That's what it's like inside those planes that simulate zero-G's for astronaut-trainees. Awesome. It is also awesome that the bird did not crash or get shot down. Bye forever Khost.

Bagram again. Operation Mountain Resolve as a part of the overarching Operation Enduring Freedom IV. We got set-up in some nice wooden buildings, took showers, and went to the exchange. This was Heaven. Haha. These little respites in and out of the firebases were life. Everything was fresh and easy, and you could walk with some cheer without getting cut off at the knees. Matrix Revolutions made its way to the bootleg DVD world and this was the big popular culture item for me at the moment. Matrix Reloaded was released prior to us deploying and that was the last movie I saw stateside. I had walked all the way down North Riva Ridge Loop from up near Magrath Gym where our barracks were. There were big dark clouds out and whole sky was grey from the usual east coast afternoon thunderstorms. It was black and green out like the Matrix, with raindrops and all.

We sat on the edge of the Bagram heliport portion of the airfield on the morning of our first mission. To our right was an A-Team loading up their Chinook. A "member" was chatting with us and he was talking about going, "hunting." To our right was a SEAL platoon walking out like they were going to play a quick game of pick-up: baseball hats and what seemed like personal weapons and not much else. No food or supplies or any logistics to note. Hueys waiting for them. UH-1 Hueys. Vietnam-era. Unique and versatile and a ghost of U.S. application. U.S. Navy decals.

Packs and weapons up and onto the Chinooks. Center-aisle. Up into the air. We are flying northeast to the Hindu Kush. A lower region but still the Hindu Kush. Alexander. You fly through a valley and you look out of the back of the helicopter (as my seat afforded me; I was first off of the bird) and you can neither trace the bottom of the valley or the tops of the mountains. It was sunny, too. Maybe that was it. Maybe the light washed the scene to appear this way? No. They are massive. This is the Western doorstep of the Himalayas. Mount Everest is only about a thousand miles (if that) to the east. To track someone in Afghanistan is ludicrous. We were flushing someone more than tracking. That was those other guys' job. Setting up blocking positions. Trying to canalize using the natural relief of the mountains.

We set down in a clearing. We all got on the ground and organized. We walked about two steps down the valley and stopped. Pretty much doesn't get any easier than this. Front-door service and no walking equals okay with me. No-one shot us down, no-one was waiting on the ground, and the setting was park-like and serene. A glen. A meadow. Inset in the wrinkles of Earth. To be honest, once we got our platoon position and our squad set upon the center open area to do whatever it is we were going to do at the time - standing there was like being on the set of a television sit-com. There was a perfectly fitting piece of axe-shaped wood that lay across the fast-moving stream cutting down the center of the valley that was telling of the care and conservatory diligence of the nearby denizens of these woods. It was almost too perfect. It was very plastic.

Here we were in a place where the last Westerners to visit were the British Army from a century or more ago. We were chatting about a mix of the necessary and the trivial, enjoying snacks, wearing the most modern combat utility uniform of the time, armed to the teeth, and having a museum experience. We came to discover through friendly conversation with the village chief that he was once an Afghani fighter pilot before the Soviet invasion. In the larger scope it was a very beautiful community locked high up in the bosom of God's stone garment.

I laid out my first live claymore in combat that night. Myself and one of my riflemen were set into a listening post up the hill. Very awkward setting up a claymore uphill. Not the least bit of a good idea no matter how well you think you engineer it. Sleeping facing uphill is also stupid. Enough on being set into a hillside facing up.

The next morning, I put myself out into the clearing during stand-to after we'd pulled back from our listening post. I figured it was the best thing to do. If there was something up there, we certainly weren't going to see it resting into the side of the hill. My platoon sergeant came out and asked what was on my mind? He was in general agreement about watching the high ground. The high ground in battle is everything.

Resupply helicopters came in with two large bundles of water bottles and meals-ready-to-eat (cube forms of many cases per side in each) sling-loaded from the bottoms of their hulls. Right behind this resupply bird was our ride home. Or maybe it was those birds. I don't recall specifically. It doesn't matter. It was just that burst of first world goods by way of vertical envelopment to one of the most remote places in the world delivered to people who weren't going to use it and couldn't recall it or rehaul it. All of the water and meals went to the village chief. Just like that. A sudden and massive redistribution of wealth between a village and an infantry company. An exchange of possible future credibility for forces that would follow on in the region. A chance to make friends. Diplomacy in the field. This is where many disciplines belong. In the field. Hopefully the units that came behind us were of like character and dignity to these people.

Away we went back into the air and towards Kabul to Bagram. Recovery. The last words from the mission was something about some aviator who didn't take a shot on a guy in a clearing who was grandstanding with an RPG. You can't keep up with that soap opera that is the operational picture. You should be generally aware of it as a sergeant, but if your people and your end of the deal is all squared-away, look no further and put your mind at ease and leave some room for leisure. That's what Commander's Intent is used for. I don't remember the interlude between the first mission and the second mission.

Probably watching movies. This is probably because the suck-factor went up to some obscene point on the scale on the second mission.

Pretty nice sunny morning on the airfield. Nothing much to speak of. Going to fly out and land in the mountains and then we are going to walk all night over a ridge and set up an overwatch on the village of Aranus in the next valley over. Meh. It'll be annoying and slow and what not but movement to daylight is old hash and that's just what we do. Better to be moving than sitting there all-night freezing to death. Everyone moderately happy on the bird. I will be the first one off. When the ramp went down, all I saw was white and all I felt was cold. There is no other option in mind here. There is no saying, "nah." First foot out. Nothing. Woosh. Three feet of snow. Move to the right. Move to the right. Someone is right behind you. It's so cold. Look up. Pull security. Is there anyone on the landing zone? No. Is there a sudden drop directly to your front that could send you plunging to your death? Oh wow, yeah, there sure is. Push right. Rock. Big rock. Like in the middle of a raging sea. Very apt in the moment. Nice. Behind the rock. Safe. Birds up. Oh my God it's so cold. The sun is going down. I'm wet from the heat exchange. It's going to ice over. We're going to freeze to death. There is a house over on the ridge in our intended direction. They landed another platoon over there. They are already walking up to it. From a distance it looks really nice.

Where are we? We're headed that way. Down. Stream. You know those waterslide parks with the 482-story plunge that leaves a wedgie in your DNA? Well, this is where we are. At the top of said-slide. We are hugging surfaces. Frozen physics. Back up. Go back. Up onto the tundra slope clearing that probably would have been more ideal instead the edge of doom chasm. But hey, who am I? We're not going anywhere. Radio up. Campfire. Perimeter. Night. LOOK: I know all of us have been cold before and this is no time to talk about cold or to get the measuring sticks out or anything; BUT, imagine being parked on a sheet of glass held at an angle. Everything has frozen over and it is slick everywhere you walk. We almost went running off a cliff which is still right in front of us and this slope and ice lean that way. There is no source of warmth from the sun, the air, or surface radiation. Everything that touches it is instantly depleted of its thermal energy and made equal in coldness. You are at 10,000' in the Hindu Kush of Afghanistan. The other platoon made it to the house. There is a smoke plume coming out of the chimney. The moon is bright. We are exposed. Thirty men in concentric circles dotted like coal markers. Beautiful in many respects, but equally distancing and relative to cold itself. The philosophy of freezing to death is miserable. Enough about the cold.

The next morning, we all almost got our heads chopped off as the Chinooks came to get us and then again as they dropped us off in the steeply-traversed valley overlooking Aranus. The angle of the ground nearly meeting the angle of those blades is instant death if you're mindful. Birds up. Set in. No snow. Warmer. Ugh man. The search for Osama Bin Laden and all of his lieutenants and all of that stuff is tiring, boring, and tedious. One of the more overused photographs on the Internet today is a Chinook with just its tail on the top of a house in Afghanistan picking up a PUC, or person under control. This was about 1000' below our overwatch position. It's always interesting to see what caption someone puts new to the photo or the comments (of course). Anyways, back to 2003. There was no real social media. We linked in with our adjacent units for the night and went to sleep after posting sentries.

Wake. On my feet. We're walking out today. Not sure how far to the pick-up zone. The silly nuisance of the noise of the helicopters quickly vanishes over time as you realize that this is your ride, your lifeline, and as will prove solidly soon, your protector. The helicopter is everything in modern warfare. Has been since the Korean War (1950 -1953). We walk down the face of the ridge we spent the night on. It's very green as we enter the canopy. Moss, algae green. Bright greens, wet dark greens nearer the water. The village of Aranus at the edge is nice and comparative to the village we had encountered the mission before. Another platoon from another battalion, the ones who held the house in the snow two nights before, led out in column down the valley trail, where we would hug the left facing slope for 11 kilometers (7 miles or so). I started to note trash on the trail. This instantly sends a team leader's senses into a frenzy. Who was littering? Check again? Yep, it's American trash. Man, fuck, it better not be our platoon. Thankfully, it was the lead platoon from the other unit. Totally unsatisfactory. Ugly. Senseless. On top of that, need we be the proverbial example of the unit that gets attacked for presenting themselves on the battlefield as, 'undisciplined'? That's how it goes: Given two units on a battlefield: One squared-away and one a complete shit-show. Which one are you going to attack? Why?

Along the way, the machine gunners and their teams began to feel the weight of their loads. Across the valley on the other ridge face were Afghani boys paralleling us moving with the same grace as the mountain goats that made their way into the finite world that was this hike. No enemy. Just sunshine. No snow. A bit of a walk. We came to the valley floor and the river that cut through it. There was a long plank - a single rail from which to demonstrate simple gymnastic balance that would take the perfect-stepper from one side to the other. If not, there was the snow-melt river that was shallow but moving with enough depth and speed to easily dispatch the heaviest of our men downriver with ease. One by one we went across. The acrobats of old had nothing on this demonstration of combat fitness and aptitude. It was as if I watching one of those elaborate oriental ceremonies that require intense choreography but deliver a simple storyline of character or plot. Very Kurosawa Dreams come to think of it.

But, there is always one. To no fault of his own. Had to be. It would almost be unbelievable that this bunch of grunts loaded for bear for combat, would execute a stream crossing on a narrow-gauge single track of wood with no error. We perform miracles routinely but the difficulty level was way up here. Kerplunk. There went one of the machine gunners. I was already across and he was relatively close. I kept my rucksack on like a fool. We had a real go at it. Someone took a pic of us at this moment and it's a nice memory we laugh at to this day. We laid in the sun to dry out as best we could and as safely as we could while we waited for the Chinooks. They finally came. Step on. Ramp half-way up. Door gunner at the ready. Birds up.

Up into the sky. It is late afternoon. Winter is setting in. The snow on the mountains at the highest peaks is pretty much permanent. I looked at my Suunto watch. Cruising altitude was 22,000'. It is very intense up there visually in these mountains when you are no longer blind in the valleys. Everyone was very tired. I was tired. I looked to my left. When everything is properly set into the bay of the Chinook you can see straight through into the cockpit and out of the canopy, forward as the pilot sees. The sun was pink. The snow on the mountain directly to our front was dark as night because the shadowy side was facing us. Wow, really, all of this nonsense and this asshole is going to fly us all into a mountain? I don't care. I'm too tired to care. At the last moment the bird pulled up. The peak dropped below the bottom of the canopy and the top of the mountain passed beneath us, showing herself behind us as we descended into Bagram.

Operation Mountain Resolve was done. Much ado about nothing, to be honest. Osama Bin Laden was still out there. It would be another 8 years before he would be killed. I often argue that the Global War on Terror, in particular Afghanistan, was and is an intelligence war with small direct actions. I am deeply conflicted as to why we would ignore so many firmly set philosophical points of why not to send conventional ground forces here; on why we would tackle this this way? I want to say that it is obscene and noisy and of no benefit in the conduct of this war, but that is not the case at the edge at least: The combat outpost war. Deep woods and mountains and aggressively surrounded positions in places that will honestly never see any civilized light again in our time. We had to be out here because we had to have physical presence. Accountability. But fortunes don't accrue over time for deployed armies. Sun Tzu will tell you outright in his 13 chapter pamphlet which is shorter than this book, that no country ever benefits from fighting long wars. This was going to take time. That's not good. But, we couldn't not – either. Paradox.

There was sleep and then relaxation and then anticipation of what the next move was. It took at least a few days from what I can remember to get refit and receive forward guidance on our next role. We were headed to Shkin in Paktika Province. It was currently Time Magazine's, Battle in the Evilest Place, which was/is still cool. That's notoriety.

It was a bright and shiny day in late November. We got on helicopters again and flew to the southern end of the Bermel Valley and the firebase at Shkin. It is pure high desert here. All the way to Pakistan there is nothing. It is orange and jagged and bright in the sun and bright in the moon and dark in its savagery. If at any point you were to dislodge from a vehicle in these lands, it would be a matter of moments before it was recognized that you, a foreigner, were in foreign land. Widely and rapidly recognized. Precarious at best, death more than likely. There is nothing here and the Afghans – especially the Taliban - intend to keep it that way.

We landed and ranger-filed into the high, four-walled ancient home that had been acquired by the United States sometime in the early stages of the conventional land war. It was November 23rd - our commander and his leadership team went out with the outgoing commander and his leadership team in what is known as a, "left-seat, right-seat ride" or also "right-seat, left-seat ride"... tomatoe tomato. Basically, it is a physical tour of the battlefield by commanders who are exchanging responsibility for an area of operations. Physical handshakes and signals are extremely valuable in the conduct of war. Eyes must all be present, and everyone must agree on what they are looking at. A reporter from Time Magazine was at Shkin, as was Geraldo Rivera.

Most of our platoon stayed behind as it was a leader-centric event between units. It's very quiet inside Afghani structures when there is minimal human signature within them. Just to think that for thousands of years people have traversed this landscape and all there is to show for it is a gas station at the border about 5 miles away and some impoverished farms. Still, that was good enough for the people of Paktika Province as it was anywhere else we went. I was kind of waiting for everyone to get back so the dick measuring contest could enter a new phase. It was like this at this point. Halfway between realizing that 'hey we're in combat and maybe we should act like adults'; and - the proverbial playground mentality where every session is a demonstration of poorly-planned ideas written somewhere in crayon to impress anyone who would give an audience. This smoothing-out occurs because of events like losing weapons and the general fatigue that sets in along with the new set of confidences that come with just being alive - and having just enough "story" to account for some bravado.

Shkin. Cobblestones set in the interior of what essentially looks like a bigger Alamo. The cobblestones further attest to my philosophy of the desert being a great filtration system and with just a bit of aggregation of these natural elements, an instant improvement. Piling rocks is more profound than one might think. Pile up some rocks. You'll remember it and you'll recall others if you've made them before.

There was word that the leader's recon had made contact. When the leader's recon returned, someone handed the platoon leader my squad leader's helmet, and in turn he handed it to me. The Humvee (HMMWV) that he had been driving in was blown to hell in the front right wheel and engine area forward of the cab. He would lose his leg below the knee. My platoon sergeant had sustained shrapnel wounds to his body and was Medevac'd along with my squad leader. We didn't expect our squad leader to return but we were half-expecting the PSG to make it back. Neither would return to combat.

For my squad leader, in a way, this was a blessing. He worked very hard and he was a sincere man. He bought into all of it, as we say. It was not all that reciprocal in the politics. After the weapon incident back at Orgun, I think that really drove him to a bad place. Discipline is tough on the line. I lost a team leader position as a young Soldier for a whole year once for forgetting the breach kit at a master breach event. I wasn't even aware of what that was or that the weird bag that was handed to me was a breach kit. It doesn't matter and that sting is what forges my repeated claims of expertise and professionalism. You have to be. The buck stops here. We were constantly doing weapons maintenance and PT. He wasn't listening much to us, his team leaders - either. My counterpart Deeds and I started being much more attentive to housekeeping. Something died spiritually in my squad leader somewhere during that previous time and he hunkered down and leaned in on us. The world had become toxic career-wise for him here I think, and it is in this tragedy of his leg being blown off that he went on to reclassify his job in the Army and stay in and do work he believed in. The best thing about military leadership and differences with others who might be adversely affecting you - as they are also in charge of you when you have fallen out of favor - is that you usually get a new boss at least every 18 to 24 months.

In happier times he would tell me about his time at the 7th Infantry Division when Fort Ord was still in use. He really liked Watsonville, which is nearby and where I was born. His face would just light up talking about it. He even had a story where his girlfriend was doing something shady and he ran up to her car and busted her window out while she was in it. I don't remember the reason but I do remember his reason being oddly good enough. He liked to say Daggone a lot. Most things started off with daggone, including that story. He would only use daggone when he was happy. No daggones meant trouble. I hope he's well. He (Daggone) deserves daggone happy remaining days and he has all my daggone blessings. I think Deeds would agree.

My platoon sergeant is of a different fortune here. There are a select few people who are made for the Infantry; made for the life that is a living feudal society with lords and knights and dragons. Those that buy into it so much and with such conviction that their mere energy compels you to commit to even more stringent standards of yourself than is honestly necessary in hindsight but not questioned upfront. You do it because you fear them. You must fear your sergeants or that fear must be something you have supplanted called self-discipline, in-excess of their own personal requirements. That is when you have personally raised the standard. Vertigo happens here. This is one of those men who understood small nuances like these in the behaviors of men - in close-knit quarters - with comparative Olympian athletic ability and meritorious achievements. He believed in every facet of the profession of Soldiering from the spirited Greeks on forward to the modern mechanical dagger fights. I personally never got along with him, but I never hated him, and he looked out for me. I think often about what the Army lost in that man and maybe what that man lost in the Army? My platoon sergeant in Afghanistan was an All-American in a few different ways that all lead home to the heart. I believe his son, who was just a young kid when we were in country - who played football and sent his dad videotapes of his games while we were at Khost, is now fighting in the same war his dad did. That guy is a hero. Guess that about wraps up ghosts and commitments and legacies for now.

They were gone. To be seen later. Hopefully. You guess. I mean, is it even relative to consider this out here? Not much. Leadership shifts. Up and down. Left and right. My platoon leader handed me my squad leader's bloody helmet. It went with the rest of his equipment and personal effects home. Patrols started heavy the next day. They didn't let up until almost Christmas.

You had to follow a serpentine path out of the wire at Shkin. This was to do such things as slow down potential assault troops, vehicles and-or vehicle-borne IEDs; but, it also conformed to the terrain which also wound out and down into the wadi system like a blossoming dry delta in the coil of nowhere. The first village was right beyond the first bend leading out of the Asiatic Mekong (I'm being fatuous now) that I just described. Before you get to this bend, though, you get to the wash of trash. So. Much. Trash.

One evening, right around EENT (End of Evening Nautical Twilight; dusk) we found ourselves near the border looking at the general area where the attack on the leader's recon had occurred. This is flat across one's vision, but the terrain is deeply rippled with wadis and it is wrinkled. Filled with mysteries and death in one respect, ancient and empty in another. Our platoon leader felt that a reconnaissance-by-fire would be the correct course of action. A reconnaissance-by-fire is what you do when you think something is somewhere, but you can't quite observe it, and the method of "poking the bush to see" gets tricky. In this case, he decided that he wanted to lob a few 105mm artillery shells into the area to our front.

Let's recap: Platoon leader wants to perform reconnaissance-by-fire, over our heads, originating from our rear, to land and explode to our front. If you are even 1 off at 1000m, left or right, the strike of the round will fall way off course. Let's not mention add/drop, as in the round or rounds could easily fall on us. I don't remember whether he fired one shot or a volley. I don't remember it being a volley, so one shot or two it was. Nice and easy from a cannon 5 or so miles away, with a map, a compass, and a few calculations that are easy (but must be right): Our platoon leader, a young West Pointer who was a graduate of the Bicentennial Class of 2002, performed a perfect textbook call-for-fire in combat with a real platoon. This is a bigger deal than you might think.

The only way to combat fear is to train. You must train hard and it must be relative and inventive; have depth of understanding to every person from top to bottom; and - be a continuous function of utility and familiarization – a cross-leveling of skill sets between the men, weapons, and equipment that are organic to the modern gunfight. These training iterations get pretty advanced during peacetime but they are nothing compared to the real thing. It wasn't the fact that an artillery shell just flew over our head on purpose. It was the fact that he plotted a shot and took it and successfully closed out the fire mission in front of - and for his platoon. That is a big deal in the profession of arms: to train and train by leading in combat. This is the more mature version of, "Train as you fight".

One more quick note about our PL. He was so involved in his platoon, he would just grab everyone and do magazine changes. He would do the sergeant's traditional job. This was not to spite us. He really just lived by example. He gave really good singular examples of what he expected. The artillery shot and the magazine changes. Soldiering plain and simple.

There are daydreams of these times as winter was setting in. It was shockingly bright on day patrols and it was the craving for the purple of night and twilight and our bunks that definitely signaled winter. We were in the wadis a lot. Christmas was bright even as snow fell for hours on-end, all day long. Our wounded platoon sergeant's family and our platoon leader's family sent all of us Christmas gifts. The company and the brigade command sergeant major engaged in a snowball fight where everyone went their own way with no alliances or reasoning whatsoever. Pleasantly dystopian interlude. Dystopia is no longer a fiction in the world. Cyberpunk is now. The Internet was in a small communications trailer with a dish hooked up to a gas generator in place that has never had public utilities: Ever. Snowball fights. Piss bottles piling up because we're too lazy to get all of our gear on to go to the latrine. Electric crank field phones. Encryption devices. Satellite phones. Goat meat meals. Laundry machines. Steak and lobster. Chewing tobacco.

December 30th, 2003. Saddam Hussein has been captured in Iraq. Time Magazine and Geraldo Rivera have long since slipped into distant memory. We're headed towards the Pakistan border today. A place called Mangretay and in particular a mountain referred to a Delta-4 and its ridge-like collection of smaller hills. Overcast. Dark overcast. The terrain changes as we head out of the valley, east into the hills, then pine forests, then mountains fresh with snow - wooded and clean and calling you inward. We get into a bowl of an area I guess (a depression), somewhere near the mountain range of interest. We get out and we start walking the fingers and draws of these foothills. Very steep, up and down. Tiring. 8000' altitude here. Cold. 0 to 10ish. I find an old lady's hut on the side of one of these interchanges of relief. She had bent the bough of an ancient pine tree down and pinned it to the earth at the edges to make her home. How many tears did this old lady cry in here? Did she even have such an emotion? Where was her husband? Was she ever married or is she an Old Maid? Did he get killed?

She had a teapot and a U.S. survival radio that was of the kind that gets passed out as a part of a humanitarian relief package.

It will be NYE in a few hours. Getting on and off of trucks and finding places and rallying patrol movements: This stuff takes time and gets easily blurred as you anticipate night. But here, the purple is not as comfortable anymore. Now it's dark and my fireteam is set over the crest of a shallow depression with a long slope going down into the darkness. Pine trees and rocks are abundant, so that is good as far as cover and concealment. Dig? No. Hell no. Pile rocks. Push down a bit.

Then I hear first sergeant and the platoon leader. Ugh. Haha. I don't care who you are in the junior noncommissioned officer world, you know damn well that in the middle of doing things, the last guy you want anywhere near you is the first sergeant. You hear him and immediately think: Dude.Go.The.Fuck.Away.

"Sergeant Lombardy," murmured loudly first sergeant through the anti-purple. "Come here."

Shuffle up.

"Sergeant Lombardy, why are you down there," asked First Sergeant?

Because man, if anything goes down, making my squad and myself into silhouette range targets is not cool.

"I'll move them back up," I said. Honestly, you don't even want to start.

"C'mon, Lombardy, let's use some common sense," said First Sergeant.

If we did this, we would be in a lot of trouble First Sergeant.

You would have to be secret squirrel friends with him to talk to him this way. He didn't have friends. Therefore - you didn't talk to him this way. Especially not Soldiers. Just like the Command Sergeant Major, they didn't subscribe to friends. People were subordinate, peer, or superior - to some degree, characteristic, or otherwise. There were no friends. It is unbecoming. Friends reek of corruption in an army. Only the chain of command and NCO support channel are your "friends." Only doctrine is your "friend." Leaders are pressed further into Service and friendship comes later.

I moved us back up a few feet. Link in left and right. Set up watch cycle. There was a fire on a hill to our back over our right shoulder as if set into the defense. We're going up there tomorrow. Someone is up there, and they don't care who knows. This is something to pay attention to. But yeah, there they are and the next morning came and there we went.

The next morning we had breakfast in the assembly area which was comprised of our second platoon, who was task-organized as the drivers and gunners and overall ground transportation mechanism for Bravo Company 1/87. Their trucks (Humvees) were in a wagon circle and first sergeant and the headquarters troops dished out a breakfast I think. Maybe not. Maybe this is illusory now. Pretty sure we ate. First Sergeant fed his troops. Him showing up in the middle of the night in the fire cuts of Louisiana back before deployment with a blueberry pancakes breakfast while we were training through night - was legend to my belly.

Afterwards, we lashed our rucks to the trucks and did what infantrymen do in assembly areas, and that is assemble tactically in the direction of the line of departure. The base of the mountain, Delta

4, was around 8500'. It was all up from here. The command sergeant major joined us. It was his duty to make his way from company to company throughout our area of operations and he was probably the most expert man in the Bermel Valley at the time. He went to the guy in the front of me and asked him for some water in his usual manner.

"Hey, Joker, let me get some water," Haha. He never carried his own water which was neat. Basically, it was his way of inducing a parasite in the economy so that everyone was aware of their own personal supply and logistics. I also took note for the first time that whenever he stopped, he did so behind a tree or rock. Almost always. It's kind of funny until you take into account that he was the chalk three leader in Gothic Serpent (Black Hawk Down), he's been shot at numerous times. There is a positive relationship between men who have been in real shooting matches and men who only dream of this day: The more you have seen, the more you act like you have seen it and it's with great care and caution. I am not even shy about ducking. Honestly, I'm not sure whether he liked the book or the film of Black Hawk Down. Colonel (then Captain) Steele was famously against the book and film. Our CSM did have an appreciation for the Cormac McCarthy quote from Blood Meridian which prefaces Mark Bowden's book. He admired it so much he had it painted on the classroom wall back at Fort Drum before we left: The same classroom he gave us a dire warning in before leaving,

"If you haven't seen combat you can thank God!" It was very out of the norm for him to raise his voice - much less yell - so it stuck. Every man in that room was a world champion at the clapback. No-one said anything back. The man didn't need flair. He embodied the virtues of war completely. He was virtuous. That means a lot in the company of professional Soldiers. It's the standard and the bar is very high, almost impossible. It has a positive correlation with understanding the high value we place on human life as Americans. We practice a high degree of discretion as the largest body of applied ethicists in the world. He was always one better and not remotely arrogant. He cared. That is all I'm really trying to say.

The first time a bullet cracks the air over your head in training is a very neat thing. I spent my first four years as a rifleman in the Marine Corps. The Marine Corps uses a butt-system where you go down range and pull the targets up and down on a pulley system called "Butts". The shooters fire, the bullet strikes the berm (usually), you pull the target down, mark it, paste any holes, and send it back up for the next shot. It's a very nice system and allows you to understand what bullets are like on the receiving end without getting hurt. The first time a bullet whizzed by me in combat was a combination of a nice sunny day near the bottom of Delta 4 after just getting going, that memory of the rifle range butts, and a nice inventory of where I should take my memorable ass next, so I can avoid the last thought,

You never hear the bullet that hits you.

I moved to a large rock. We were on a main finger leading to the top and I was on the right side of the bell curve. I took account of my fireteam and we were all nearby. I just hoped that no-one got shot because if someone went tumbling, it would be miserable getting them back up. First thoughts: Accountability and consequences.

Next, you know what? This rock is alright. I'm going to take my first moment to thank God just because. The word got down to us that first platoon was in contact near the crest. I guess the fire pit guys had stayed around.

Were these guys that 1st platoon met surprised that we came up the hill? Did they die surprised? Or, were they up there and in typical ancient world fashion, with much courage but little sense, hoping to find glory?

We're moving back up the hill. It takes a while. I hear helicopters. Stop. Move. Check men, weapons, and equipment. Use the radio. Move and communicate are covered. Is shoot next? Eventually we end up on the crest. It was very beautiful on top of Delta 4. Clear, sunny, snow on the hill, the green of the trees contrasted with the blue of the sky and the black rock; up ahead I could see our commander and his antenna farm. The man who would become the Great Geometer in a couple of hours was consolidating and reorganizing and preparing to move his company down the mountain. The Great Geometer to me at least. The first platoon had killed three men along with help from Marine Cobras on station. That was it. It was done, and we were moving on. The commander's antenna farm varies in size and composition depending on mission requirements. Today he had a future Medal of Honor winner and his radio operator with him who served as our forward artillery observers, plus the company RATELO (radio telephone operator; radioman), and the Air Force JTACs (Joint Tactical Air Controllers: the guys that call in air support). This little group takes a great burden off of the commander and they are THE most sacred pod in the whole company. Those men are some of the most important in modern warfare. Protect your officers, your radio operators, and your machine gunners. Those are the first three I look to kill on a battlefield and I learned that from reading about the Viet Cong. Add protect your tactical air controllers because they are a hot mix of all 3 that we can no longer live without. It is a very stoic thing to encounter on a mountain top.

Ice whipping in breezes, the crystal clouds kicking up, men kneeled and huddled tightly conferring their information as needed: antennas sprouted up: Some fully extended, and some tied down; some folded up with only that part extended which was necessary to catch static. The poets of applied communication and sovereign soft power until lightening bolts are required.

Standing on top of Delta 4, one of our machine gun team members came over to me and asked if I had anything to eat. I just happened to have a pork chop in Jamaica sauce MRE main meal in my left trouser pouch pocket. Pre-heated from the climb. Food can always be found on me in the field. I gave him the package and joked for a minute with him before we started our walk down to some lower hills respectively named Delta 3, 2, 1, etc.

The sun was falling fast now. Everything was breezy. We were moving steadily and would be at the trucks in no time as long as no-one got any bright ideas on either team, if you know what I mean? I was looking forward to putting caffeine back in my system and letting my body rest by the potbelly stove. Maybe throw some salt on top of her and cook an aluminum foil wrapped MRE main meal or two. All the good stuff. When I am smoked and haven't ingested anything other than the random protein or grain or fruit/vegetable I start to daydream. These are always fascinating and like a lot of things, I press a bit hard on my heart and mind every time I run across a daydream that manifests into some integral reality. What I saw was four to seven shadows sprinting to the right as if to tactically move positions, hastily. I say four to seven because that is kind of allowing for criss-crossing shadow figures if you will. Counting one as two or two as one. I drew my rifle up as play, loosely looked through my ACOG from a useless eye-relief distance, then resumed the hike without a thought. Gone as fast as they came.

The trucks. Second platoon was in a wagon circle waiting for us. We got on our trucks and lost all discipline. What you are supposed to do is tactically mount up and immediately pull security and prepare to move at the ready. What happened was a bunch of dicks got on the circus wagon and pulled out their snivel gear (the clothes that keep you warm) and woobies (poncho liners – greatest thing ever made) and started huddling up, not too concerned about anything. I sat on the back of the truck where I always sat, driver side. The first sergeant came trooping the line and he was pissed everyone was dicking the dog, but at the same time it came out half-assed and forgiving. Even Rangers have the occasional empathetic moment. Don't tell them I said that though and if you're in the Army and reading this: Don't try this at home. :)

I had two SAW Gunners. The squad automatic weapon, or the M-249 SAW, is an amazing light machine gun designed for the American Infantry. They are beautiful machines capable of horrible things in the right hands. When I say, "right hands," I mean only competency in employing the weapon system: not us or them; good or evil; or the like. One stood up and manned his SAW facing forward over the driver's cab. The other was seated across from me. As long as him and I were on our mark, looking past us for more stuff to pick at was not sensible to anyone who may be trooping the line. The first glance is important in any inspection. We were semi-squared-away, and I gave my usual smile to first sergeant which he always treated as suspicious. Haha. Who, us? Nooooo. Have a nice evening, First Sergeant!

I only remember getting going, convoy-wise, looking over my shoulder to the front to see one of the big, over-laden, over-decorated trucks headed into the mountains flashing its lights towards us; then - hearing word about an ambush. Strange voices by local radios and from inside the vehicle cabin; chatter between driver, tactical commander, and radio. The phenomenon of it getting dark seemed to speed up looking at headlights. Definitely messes with any night vision adaptation: natural, mechanical, or otherwise. It is quite common to not even mess with night vision or think about the surrounding night when bright lights are in the vicinity. It's a false comfort zone. Then the trucks were past us. We were moving down into a wadi cut by natural water flows. Over time this trench came to be about 10 feet across and four feet deep with parallel non-stepped vertical faces. Basically, no amount of 4-wheel drive was getting a vehicle out of this canal once set into it and driving forward: Especially with 20 vehicles or so and assuredly one or two to be locked up behind you. It was straight through. So, if there was someone, the order was push on and don't stop. Still, I don't remember being all that worried. I wasn't convinced of anything other than the pot belly stoves of Shkin.

Back in Khost while on the perimeter of FOB Salerno, the art of making MRE bombs had taken on a period of cultural renaissance. An MRE bomb has a variety of versions. MREs come with a green bag (chlorine green) and a heater that has some foundational structuring in charcoal and whatever else makes it burn. You slip in what you want to heat up, which is also in a foil packet that is air-tight and packed with so many preservatives and calories: Everything a Soldier needs. Into the green clear sleeve, add water up to a certain dotted line, fold the excess flap over, set into the box that the meal-foil-packet came in, and place at a slight lean of 15 degrees. Let boil.

Now, with the proper modifications to said- process, you can place the boiling water and expanding air bag in a state of excess pressure and after adding oh say, Tabasco Sauce, you can induce chemical warfare on your companions without mercy by detonating said device in a myriad of time-delay strategies. It's a homemade stink bomb with pepper flavor.

To reorient right-quick: We are a light infantry company of the 10th Mountain Division with around 100 men. We have 20 or so vehicles, mostly HUMVEES, all with some heavy machine gun or at least a guy with a SAW mounted topside. We have an MP (Military Police) detachment that includes at least two female sergeants that helped with female engagement of the indigenous Afghan women. You have to believe that we take care of business in the most expert and professional manner at the edge of strife. We have two Marine Cobras on-station. There is a lot of firepower and know-how making locomotion out of the mountains but ultimately made obedient to the terrain that called itself our road home that evening. We are heading from the east which is Pakistan, westward back into the Bermel Valley of Afghanistan by way of a foothill village known as Mangretay.

I am seated on the back of the truck-bed of an open back Humvee. I am on the driver side rear wheel well utilizing the edge of the wooden planked bench that stretched a length on both sides of the bed. We are rolling through the wadi and it is the usual chaotic bump and jolt, banging your ass to death. You never know how much you appreciate smooth pavement streets until you have literally not seen one in five months. My other SAW gunner was seated opposite of me. Upon entering the actual village of Mangretay, I noticed that all of the lights were off in all of the houses. Afghans are festive gatherers in the evening - always. The valley began sloping up to my left almost immediately beyond the buildings. To my right though seemed to be a purple plain that indicated farmlands and flatland leading a bit out to the right up-slope of the valley. The vertical faces on the right were more extreme than what seemed to be gentle but progressive slopes to the left.

POP.

MRE bomb? Really? I dunno. The thought I had mirrored that three-stage sentiment. I was tired and uncaring of the surroundings. Placid in knowing we were headed back. And just like that so went the tick marks of the next ten seconds or so. Maybe it was less. Time dilation is an art form in description that may be lacking here, but the next few things happen pretty damn quick:

The pop was an IED that maybe fizzled? But it was distinctly marked by the sudden induction of tracers followed by the sound of gunfire, en-masse. Someone or some device had tripped an ambush. Light travels faster than sound. I look up and sit up in like motion and my head cants slightly up and to the left where I am met with the vision of a red tracer headed straight for me. Like a hot flash and pop that suddenly infused their properties - registering their presence in my gourd, the bullet passed to my left just off to the left of my helmet near my eyeline. Diverge with me here: In the first sense, I think that that bullet passed almost centerline but leftward down the truck bed where two men are seated on the bench behind me - and one is standing directly above the middle of the cab. In the second parallel sense, and the very overwhelming realization that forced my mouth open loudly but extremely humbled,

"Holy shit I almost got shot in the head."

Like some crazy parakeet, my SAW gunner across the way, cawed out like some raven,

"YOU GOT SHOT IN THE HEAD??!!" Honestly it was squeaky and funny in hindsight. Just trying to preserve our dignity.

I simultaneously replied, "NO, RETURN FIRE!!" (this is honestly the shittiest fire command ever given in fire team leader history lol) and raised my rifle directly back down the path of the tracer. I have a firm grasp of applied calculus. I understand motion, instantaneous rates of change - the areas under curves: all of it in real world application. I have a gift for hand-held instruments and the gun just happens to stand neck and neck for my soul with my writing tools. Put the two together, and time and space become antique and approachable. As the commotion of my fire team coming to life erupted around me I laid in my general gunline. I didn't even send my eye to the sights. I knew where I was going with my gun-lay and I understand triangles. I half... no I fully expected to not make it to that moment where I returned fire. If I had been that Afghani that fired on me, I assure you I would have followed up with lead rounds until I made my mark, which should have been directly thereafter. However, for whatever reason, there was no other rounds my way. I sent five rounds back in a few seconds.

It wouldn't be until in an olive grove a couple of weeks later that I would reconcile whether I killed that man or not. It didn't matter at the moment except for the fact that no more rounds were coming my way - at least from that direction. Meanwhile, everyone behind me is okay and everyone in the truck is up and scanning and-or shooting.

My fear of that bullet having hit someone behind me was alleviated. I started looking around and taking accountability; pretty scared that that the guy might show back up; OR - that at arm's length on the berm of the wadi would be someone that someone else up ahead may have missed. There was someone and then he was down. He was shot by the fire team ahead of us. That was Deeds' team. Then the Hummer stopped. Wait, why aren't we driving? Oh man, I hope the driver isn't shot. Against any good sense, I hopped off really quick to check the driver. All of the sudden he was telling me to get back in. Oh good you're not shot.

There was a heavy machine gun on the right side of the valley. As stated, the right side stretched out across farmlands and then shot straight up a vertical face. It was here that the Marine Cobras came back into our cognizance and being. This was a magic bubble of time and space: We were in the middle of an ambush. There were tracers and rounds flying in all directions. There were Taliban at arm's length intermittently along the convoy, and there was a large machine gun raking the whole valley and kill zone arbitrarily. We were all awake and alert and checking each other by calling out names for instant response and assurance after the mad minute that kicked everything off.

The Great Geometer. The whole of my panel on Afghanistan in any state of reflection always centers around our company commander. There is only this man at this moment in time and this moment in time was the most important in terms of consequences. At no point in time again would the entire company of men be in immediate danger of suffering catastrophic damage leading to combat ineffectiveness, ever. It was very possible. I was not near our commander. This was the story passed down directly thereafter, in the time when we would be collecting our senses around pot belly stoves - a couple of hours in the future.

The Great Geometer got his name from me, and its usage (as of the authoring of this manuscript) is unique to me. It comes from what boils down to this man rationalizing his situation and reducing it to the best and simplest approximation of reasoning and language to express what he may or may not need from the Marine Cobras for the sake of the lives of the men of his company. There was a large machine gun, .50 caliber, raking the kill zone, which we were all in. The valley was an arbitrary expanded space of death. Like Roombas with a Terminator upgrades, the Marine Cobras asked for the front-line trace or general positioning of troops. There was probably chatter about the big gun. What shined through was that The Great Geometer knew that all of his people were together, in a line. He made a simple linear approximation and communicated it with an immediate visual reference that would coordinate literally hundreds of steps of logic and reasoning (and possibly bloodshed) in one fell swoop,

"We are all on the road."

You can see this, even if you have no grasp of the scene being described. That is Euclid. That is foundational point-line-plane geometry: The root of western logic and of mathematics as an art of pattern and proof, and thus verification. A lot of talk about mathematics being the queen of the sciences, but as number theory is her queen, Euclid is king. Every mathematician after 300BC is a descendant of Euclid. This well-constructed and unbroken path of royal purple is still a gift to men who will listen. With this set of variables defined to all whom mattered, we kept driving down the road struggling to stay at intervals and yet together and out of the kill zone and valley and to get out and away from the village of Mangretay in general.

The Marine Cobras were suddenly visible against the right valley wall. Have you ever seen True Lies where Schwarzenegger pilots the Harrier up the face of the skyscraper to the floor where the antagonists are located and then he just hoses everything and everyone on the n-th floor? One of the Cobras stood on overwatch while the other made its way to the base of the terrain and raised up - pausing, then unleashing a fury of 20mm cannon and rockets forward into the Taliban. It was here that time resumed and everywhere within earshot was a burst of cheer. It was as if we had just watched an Olympic moment unfold and be definitively enclosed in a breath of modulated medieval fire: Daggone modern mechanical dagger fights. We appreciated this moment like the actors of Homer did before returning to, "PULL SECURITY!" Not sure what that translates to in Greek?

We stopped in the forest at the far end of the village that would take us out into the open valley. I got off of my truck. I visited my team members and then just stood there in the dark, quiet. Standing. The green glitter of my night vision more dazzling than normal because of the adrenaline. Then my balls dropped. Like I was 13 again. I couldn't even at this moment. My balls had literally taken leave and just returned. But that was it. I could tell you about the drive out and all, but it is nothing but more poetics.

The next morning, first and second platoon went back to the village and arrested every fighting age male and took assessment and accountability of what they could. I was pleasantly surprised that we got to stay back. I spent New Year's Day sitting in the sunshine outside of the team leader hut and smoking cigarettes and drinking coffee.

My friend had sent me a letter about some show he watched about the contracting and development of the F-22 and the F-35. I read that. One of my fellow sergeants had a hard-bound, green-colored copy of The Wealth of Nations by Adam Smith. I read a bit from there. All the good stuff.

Inventory the night before had developed into an accountability issue as some of the men's equipment, including a tripod and some gun stuff (but no guns), had been lost during the fight. It didn't take long for video from the Taliban fighters themselves to make its way onto Al-Jazeera and back to us at Shkin. It included footage of them preparing for us to pass back through, the tracers at a distance when the ambush kicked off, and the morning after before we returned. They had been standing in the wadi, giving praises to Allah; our gear and shit everywhere on Taliban shit-talking videos. BUT, "Look, we are on TV. Like that is us. In a war, in an ambush. That is our enemy that we just fought videotaping us." We were now another episode in the infinite struggle known as war and it smelled of commercial authenticity. It felt like attainment and a permanent freedom from the also repeatedly asked,

"Have you been to combat?"

Practice, test, answers - all complete. What's next? Let's do this. Let's fight this war. What's for dinner?

I refer to Afghanistan and Iraq (and any of the regional interests we have assumed responsibility for in our quest to fight the Global War on Terror) as agora wars. Our enemy is not forming up on the Plains of Troy to push Greeks back into the sea in the traditional manner. This is a war of financiers: Buccaneers of the Market. Terrorists and their cells need civilization to take hold, manifest, and ultimately look to turn.

Revolutions begin in the home. Everything is market oriented in the engagements; the market is everywhere; you are a subset of this market and the one that followed you to the other side of the world. Our videogames and fast food are coming right behind us, no matter what. This is commerce, engagement of economic resources, and ultimately - struggle to obtain and develop these logistics so as to effect stability and reintroduce civic objects from initial governance to infrastructure. To exert influence by economic means has very much been the modality of our fight from the minute we gained enough battlespace to conduct the first consolidation and reorganization, theater-wide. We are money. Everything about each of us as individuals just flourishes with the notion of opulence in the eyes of our foreign hosts. We have now, by the millions, entered these theaters as individual ambassadors and touched a hundred lives easily in our own person just by executing moderate acts of kindness on patrols. Giving water and supplies where they were allocated; a piece of candy or an entire bag for the local kids; establishing communications with local leaders to open up resources and ease neighborhood strife. All of it very dignified and heartfelt work. You can never really rationalize allowing these people to go backwards but you also realize that sooner or later they would have to step up and make a go at it. More than likely they will not. A people ruled by religion is not progressive and that is the state of Afghanistan.

The markets in Afghanistan are dusty towns. There is an American pastoral country-western kind of feel to these towns and their agoras. But - without the peculiar North American spirit per-se. The Spirit of '76 however seems to be present in its most rugged people in the remoteness to which we are sent, and this is overtly pleasing. They really live freedom. You can see how hard freedom can be if you don't want to enfranchise – or can't. Osama Bin Laden couldn't enfranchise – or so he claimed – and gave this as a profound reason for his jihad. We do carry a spirit with us. Along with agora wars comes the new tactical battle drill: The Mall Shopper. It's the art of showing up ready to deal death and simultaneously pretend to admire the goods or smuggle a lull to make a purchase. It's a strange art. Our enemy does it naturally. With the death of the consumer mall in the United States, you can almost see some derivative of this now as new capitalists move on the land and property and those that aren't snatched up are populated by the displaced - and mapped into the dystopian. Same effect here. A land of squatters. A land where this is a normal way of life. A life-long rite of passage. Place to place. Slowly, with care. Squatting is not about loitering so much as it is about preserving every bit of energy they have.

Everything became easier after January had made its debut. In terms of not knowing what direct combat looked like or felt like, everything became easier. My nuts had dropped, and I walked normal again. I had a bit of a lean and a swagger. It was very much a confident, almost business suit feel. It was pretty great. We were all smiling on the inside and everything made sense and there was no more pretentious "what-if"-in and no-one was too interested in trying to snuff his brother with MRE bombs or duct-tape birthdays. Okay, I'm stretching a bit. If you had a birthday and it was known while in theater, you usually got sacked in the middle of the night, taped to your cot (always done within main base activities and never on patrol) and made into a postmodern sundae: a fine concoction of left-over chow.

We were out one evening headed into a defensive posture somewhere up ahead. We had stopped in a column along one of the dirt roads. I was standing at the back of my vehicle enjoying the reprieve from the constant ass-banging we got riding in the Humvees. Five months of no paved roads has its effects. I turned around and saw Mars Bars and Jersey K. Fashizzle (we'll just call them that, they'll know who they are. haha) and I think Deeds, my fellow team leader, was back there along with maybe two or three others. I walked towards them nonchalant and as I got closer, their expressions and voices dampened until I got almost right up on them - when one (it was either Deeds or Mars Bars) gasped, and with that gasp everyone else backed him up in a choral uuuuuhhhhh,

"Jesus, Sergeant Lombardy....," said one or the other, "We thought you were sergeant major.",

The command sergeant major and I did have like-builds and manners and for once, a comparison was made to another person that didn't sting or stink. My last name is Lombardy. Do you know how many times I have had to disassociate myself from the Vince Lombardi bloodline? Ha. I would probably like football more if this phenomenon were not so persistent over forty-plus years.

We remounted our vehicles and headed into an olive grove for the night. A warning order had been issued for the following morning that regarded moving to contact on a gas station somewhere nearby in the valley. I was feeling good. The weather was nice. What little chill there was seemed to ease right off with our special silk underwear making everything wearable and sleek and thermostatic. Is thermostatic the right word here? Is it even a word? I'll leave this here as a reminder that I am/was a Soldier; a career, professional Soldier, and to those Soldiers that read this: It is okay to just sound things out and make-due with what you have language-wise if you have a story to tell. On top of the point I want to make here about not to worry about your language skills, I want you to know that your story doesn't have to be about the heroic or a major event or anything else. It can be like this: In one's lane and a memory sign for it. As long as it is an honest effort, it doesn't matter - and is worth defending for passing down to at least one or two members of your posterity. Language is perfected over time. Memory deserves care but you only have so much time. Future Soldiers need to hear grunt level voices. Experience makes the birth of wisdom possible.

To reinforce my point, there are two difficult portions of this two-war tale that I have reconciled time and again; I have warred with their telling; I have found them resolved but likewise unsettled and sometimes nagging for my attention. One of them was on this evening in this olive grove and so as to not mince words, has to do with Satan in the generalist Christian sense. A presence that was unsettling in the least. It could have been an Angel if these things do exist. There were reports of people seeing Angels at the Flight 93 crash site in Pennsylvania. I mean, Angels are kind of scary if they want to be. Deeds and I pulled first watch. I think we were doing two-hour shifts in pairs and we decided to pull rank and both share the first slot so we could sleep the rest of the evening uninterrupted. There are few things more unbalanced and startling than being woken up for guard in the middle of the night and then trying to get back to sleep; or, getting the second to last shift. The last guard shift is okay because you are all ready to go when everyone wakes up and that is always a plus. But the second to last is bullshit. You get to a point where sometimes you don't even wake the next shift and just coast the rest of the way to wake up and stand-to. I'm drifting. This is because, like I said, I really am spent on how to tell this but the idea of it and the memory of it has not left since, so it should be here.

I was feeling good, as noted. Aloof. First two hours of guard with Deeds? Nice evening, no inclimate weather; no real threat seemed unmanageable. Life is good. Let's do this (again). First hour down, the second hour came. By the time the second hour began I was doubled-over on my knees, low to the ground. I had suddenly been overcome by the same sickness I had in the guard tower back in July in Bagram. But this was different. I was very much constrained to the moment and I immediately thought about the ambush on New Year's Eve and my would-be assailant dead from my own response? Who was this person who was standing over me wearing Deed's combat boots? 'Deeds wasn't standing there at that moment,' is as flat and plain as I can state. I grew a bit scared. This was Deeds standing there and I was just stressed and sick and it was probably either the malaria medication, the food, or it was evil as a headliner. Shaytan in Arabic or its Dialects.

The next morning, I woke in the olive garden, alone. Very alone. More alone than I probably should have been but grateful for the fact our new platoon sergeant had seen it my squad leader's way and let me remain behind. It took me a while to get out of my bag, but when I did, everything was grey. The trees were grey. The sky was grey. The ground was just grey flaky dusty stone. Then a huge splash of color. Five or six Taliban wrapped in super-bright colored quilts, bound loosely, and guarded by our military police detachment standing inside a circle of concertina wire. This is all I see. No-one should be this alone in Afghanistan unless on purpose and trained for such. I am reasonably well trained as are my companions but I am also a member of a line infantry unit and this liberty is not the norm. I absorbed the moment because it was spectacular in its matte grey and striking pool of color. Even the enemy had color in the moment. In fact, only the enemy had color in the moment. Was this that apparition's calling card? I don't know. The company returned later in the day and I rejoined my fireteam. Nothing else was said and my pallor was sufficient I think to keep such questions at bay. I got well, quick. It was all seamless. Like nothing happened. For all I know, nothing did happen except I got sick and delirious. But it wasn't like that then, and it doesn't come any other way when I reminisce. I have spoken with Deeds before about this, a few times since.

We had a phase of patrolling where we skirted the western edge of the valley and here were dragons. Dragon spines were steep, jagged, massive ridges that extended to the south end of the valley, and what I like to refer to as dragon heads at the north. The dragon heads I speak of were the stone fortresses carved into the sheer cliff faces in the northwest end of the Bermel valley. Some of them carved and constructed thousands of years ago and inhabited by untold generations of Afghanis, Bactrians, Persians, and all of the Empires that have found their predicament to be here and with these people. Their eyes were rectangular.

In this northwestern region of the valley since I am naming things in dragon terms, we hooked up into some of the villages that were more remote up and beyond the high walled fortresses and cliffs. These you could say were dragon wings. The land was a plateau here now that I think back. Snow was still here, and the slant of the land was smooth and lensing as if to be planar and the surface of a flapping wing all at once. We stopped one evening here and there were cervices that ran venous and circuitous across the high valley floor. Mini-wadis if you will? Big cracks in the stone more like it. The sky was clear, and all of the grey of winter was slipping away. The grey of the olive grove was still there, but there was no fear. Just a reminder as spring was making its way to Central Asia. When night came, the stars came. I don't even want to get into a "how beautiful the stars were" measuring contest but it was like standing on a platform at the edge of the universe and it was mind-boggeling in its portrait to me. Most of us had set our gear and bags into the crevices that connected buddy teams and that is where I went: Into this most convenient bosom of the earth for a temporary rest. I pulled my neck gaiter up and my poly-fabric beanie cap (snivel gear) down over my eyes and breathed heavy into my sleeping bag, face covered, and now a tactical cocoon in the middle of nowhere.

I shaved my head figuring it would be just right by the time we left. A few shaping haircuts and a good high and tight would be reformed in time to return to garrison, left, abreast, and in-step. A few final snows hit us and we were fortunate enough to be shut down for a bit and that left us with long afternoons to mill about and watch movies, play games, and catch up on sleep. A friend and former fellow team leader from another platoon whom I will simply refer to as the Dungeonmaster, had written to Wizards of the Coast – TSR, and asked for whatever Dungeons & Dragons materials they would be willing to donate to him and his fellow Dungeoneers. This was the time when the confidence in the war was probably at its peak, if there ever was such a period. I say this because it was opulent for us as Soldiers. People just gave us stuff. Whatever we wanted or needed or had no business having. It was there. This is contrary of course to the fact that it is propped up against the megalith of war financing and is systemically dependent upon it. However, when the floodgates are open between an army and the people that it serves and that relationship is profoundly proud and respectful in both directions, it is magical and not a day goes by where some comfort could not be obtained. This is unheard of in the history of warfare: Never before has a more free-wheeling, democratic, caring, and sufficiently groomed body of warriors ever presented itself for long-standing combat in a more poignant fashion than the United States has done and continues to do in the modern era. We are chíc. That's the word for it. And with that came the Dungeonmaster's giftings from Capitalism: A complete of set of rule books, dice, and such. If you know of these products, you know they are finely made and expensive. Dungeonmaster is now a sergeant major as of the authoring of this book. Games are important to warfare. The Dungeonmaster was at home on multiple levels here and it was great to see him running games late into our snowy evenings. I imagine this is what it looks like when his first sergeants have to go see him. I bet it's always a good game with him and his team: Stuff like this makes better people. It's good economics.

Snowstorms were frequent. We planted a sensor field one afternoon when we first got here. It was a ways off by Adam's hill. We walked out there in these blizzards from time to time if one of them signaled movement and then again to recover them. Passive warfare and transient techniques in the heart of an Afghan winter. Laying traps. Recovering traps. Simple sensors. Plain radio transmission. GPS. Signals disappearing the same as the unknown walkers off into the blizzard. The arrays weren't complex enough to determine direction of travel I don't think.

Rangers had moved next door to Shkin composed as Task Force 121. Their camp was built anchored off of the jailhouse. I don't remember if I noticed this small group of buildings before 121 moved in or if it wasn't until we became actively involved in coordinating patrols and guarding prisoners as a part of a joint sharing of assets and division of labor. This was the only time while in Afghanistan that I was inside one of their jails. It's bad enough that it's a jail. It's even worse that it's in Afghanistan. And, it is beyond imagination in the human sense of dignity what it would be like to be a prisoner in this jailhouse in the Bermel Valley with no U.S. or Allied western armies to intervene on an abuse and nothing even remotely available in terms of legal representation that we have available to us as Americans. Honestly, it's not a jail. It's a slave hold. That cobblestone building had been around for a long time. How many fates ended in here? How many horrors occurred inside this dark pocket of stones? Also, how many different uses have been made for that building over the years? You could effectively put farm animals and store grain and such as well inside; but, the bars were there, and the cell divisions defined the utility of the facility. The Afghan guards would come in and beat on the bars. None of the men in the cells moved. No groans. Nothing. Huddled facing with their backs to the bars. Dark. Cold. Snow still on the ground in patches outside. Walking away from that compound was always a relief. There's a lot of military pun in that last sentence. 'Pun'itentiary kind of stuff. Nice way to end a segment on a jail.

We patrolled again near where our scouts had been killed. We would spend time near lthe town of Shkin and its one gas station at the entryway to Pakistan. Everything became bright again, but more importantly, yellow bright. The dirt was no longer covered in snow or patched with icy mud puddles: It was dirty yellow; the contrast between sky and ground; the hint of spring; this is the first and probably last thing that becomes apparent here: that the beauty of Spring can exist in that essence interleaved with the upcoming killing season. The Afghan men were congregating openly. Mostly to talk about trade; but - this is the land where grudges last 40 years and there is a planned and deliberate murder cycle that goes with these debates. If you are old and have a beard as an Afghan male, this is a mark of a life carefully lived. No matter what goods and services the agora brings, war always follows. Here the Taliban would enter these realms to cull the skim or outright seize the town or parts of the town whenever their God required it of them. As Sun Tzu stated plainly, one unit of enemy supplies is worth ten of ours. These men were light fighters of the highest caliber. They knew all of the tenets of mobility even if probably only a scatter of any of them ever knew who Sun Tzu was. War is permanent. A prime number of the species. It exists, and its tenets are postulates, unmoved by time, and alien in origin. If we evolve and return to the stars, we will take war with us. It is mutable, and the facets of war can be used to develop intricate and mighty applications of the human experience, but it is still war. This gets lost philosophically both on armies and the people they serve.

Back in my lane I was sitting on a ledge in the southern end of the valley about five miles from the patrol base at Shkin. We were inspecting a schoolhouse. Another normal building to many of us. But just like the jail, no matter how bright it was outside, this wasn't a place of righteous construction. What was taught here? Fundamental Islam surely. But, that's not the problem. The problem is that it was the only thing that was taught. There is no measure for success in such a pedagogy - and with that, no empowerment of the student. No hope. This wasn't a school, it was an indoctrination center from which countless generations of kids entered and left - maybe, because surely some students paid their tuition in Sharia currencies - never to see the light of a civil day: Only the Bermel Valley. Forever.

I hear the familiar crack. Someone is shooting at me. I was really tired on this day. I remember it because I was so exhausted that I just sat there even after the realization. I probably already mentioned but the Taliban generally aren't very good marksmen. This set in along with the exhaustion and helped me to continue my war plan of staying parked on my ass as long as possible. I could see my team and the platoon was finishing up. As I turned to let someone know on my ICOM I took another second to listen (or wait to be struck). It was gone. The platoon rallied to move out and I had relayed the phenomenon, but it was no blood no foul at the moment. No-one was chasing ghosts anymore.

Night Vision and the Pepsi Can. Without trying to harangue the gods of war for more contrast and comparison, the culture that we are as Soldiers values ingenuity. One night, headed back to Shkin from the southern end again, my night vision battery cap contact broke off as I was moving to get everything operating. Night was falling. We weren't very far from post but that doesn't matter. I have to see. I need my night vision. It is irresponsible to let this lull without trying to correct it. Most accidents occur within a few miles of the home. You wear your seatbelt no matter how far you are moving the car. The same goes with the table of organization and equipment. Bells and whistles or get the fuck out. Pepsi can. Produced in Central Asia. Probably a factory in Saudi Arabia. I don't know. But, what these cans have that ours don't is the old school peel-back aluminum tab. This tab could work. Git 'er done. I ripped off the tab, took a sip, poured out the rest as the Humvee bumped and banged our asses with no let-up. Then, I placed the tab in the well of the battery cap and as gyroscopically balanced by tough leg muscles as I could be, I placed the cap onto the battery compartment. Locked it into place. Flipped the switch. Green. Green glitter light.

Almost everyone had taken leave home by now or visited Doha for a few days. I had not. Honestly, it wasn't worth the break in momentum. All I would think about would be what I needed to be thinking about back at Shkin. It makes for no enjoyable time with such things concerning one's heart and mind. However, someone decided that it would be cool to amend the notion of getting some R&R in along with washing the company headquarters vehicles back at Kandahar. In any other circumstance this would have brought instant rage out of me for the pegged injustice. However, here was something different. I grew a smile. A genuine smile. I was done. Get on that bird and get out and be glad.

Of all of the people selected to come back with me (along with a few others) was none other than Shoes and Biscuits. We got on the Chinook when the day came to fly back to Kandahar. I noticed something different. I was no longer the first man on the ramp. Shoes and Biscuits was where I normally sat, and I sat next to him, one-seat-space-in. He was, whether he realized it or not, buffering me; shielding me. Maybe he was doing that all along. Maybe his behavior is what kept me going and gave me what I needed to reflect on to keep focused and ultimately alive. Like I said before, he was very capable. There was no reason he couldn't do my job. He just didn't want to. I think this was his way of thanking me for putting up with his shit. He gave a deuces sign with his fingers as we lifted off and watched Shkin grow tiny in the valley. This is the way I like to remember that moment and I like it for all of the reasons in that moment. It was genuine and without pomp or circumstance.

No company command structure in sight. Wash some vehicles? Hang out in the water in the desert even if it would take several days just to clean a single vehicle of all of its mud, some of the floor wells a foot thick with earth cakes. These things had to be dust free. Seriously, it's a horrible paradox of inspection and reinspection. But here, again, no big deal. I went and bought a PlayStation, a Matrix video game for the console, some sundry items, some Copenhagen, and some coffee, and of course a Pepsi or Coke or two. I took really long showers. I worked with the others all day in the sun and water and it was clean and stress free.

Finally, we were all back together and staged inside a huge tent; expandable, inflatable hangars. Big concrete pads for floors. Smooth. No bumps on these surfaces. We all wandered around. Freshly washed men reintegrated with civilization. No coffee shop or PX was safe. Everywhere you could see headphones and the old CD bookcases. Laptops, carefully wrapped and taped to survive the harsh conditions for nine months - lost their protective garments and became commercially- and socially-acceptable machines again. But there was one figure that was different and that was our First Sergeant. Well over a year before, while at the Joint Readiness Training Center in Louisiana, I had found this man in a similar contrast. At JRTC, after many, many days of continuous training evolutions, we had finished our exercises and were all country bumpkin and rolling around on the back of big trucks, police calling the ranges. First Sergeant came walking up with the CSM and some other senior NCOs - and the Louisiana wild showed up with a light fog hugging the ground under a bright blue sky and there were these amazing brown horses of notable good health. That's what we were and these men were the jockeys. All was still and calm and okay. First Sergeant had mounted the truck and this is when I noticed that he wasn't his usual composed self. He was exhausted. It broke through every toughness and made him childlike and he was laughing and silly. He was never unbecoming, though. It was then that I noted a man that was even more resilient than my platoon sergeant had been. Our First Sergeant gave his entire being to the United States Army and to us. He was a Ranger and he was relentless at his profession. He had fought in Panama. He had done many other assignments and such long before he ever got to us and it showed in how professional he went about keeping his company of men and its colors alive.

It was here in this tent on the other side of the world, while waiting to go home, that I got a final view of his expert demeanor and character. He was sitting on the edge of his cot, his head in his hands, a copy of Stephen Ambrose's historical account of Lewis & Clark, Undaunted Courage, in his lap. No foot traffic went within 20 feet of him. There was a big aura around him that said: Do Not Disturb.

Iraq

I loaded up my Ford Taurus at our apartment in Barstow and headed to the National Training Center by way of a stop at the drive-thru at McDonald's at Barstow Station. My wife came along to bring our car home. My first wife was an Australian immigrant (British citizen) whom I had married in New York before heading to Afghanistan. There are two routes you can take up to NTC from Barstow and if you go into town, the far edge of town towards the Marine Corps Logistics Base, then the inertia says to take the newer road. The other road branches off this route up near Jackhammer Pass and lands you on Main Street near the Harvey House. Formation was set for late evening near midnight and it was dark and cold as a desert gets at night in January. There was no conversation.

Getting my stuff out of the trunk next to the blacktop I pulled my A-bags and rucksack out and slammed it shut. In this instance, she started bawling. Like an explosion of tears and such. Just a strange and abrupt display of emotion from the void. But in this moment, something struck me: I'm going to die at the back of a vehicle. I'm going to get blown up at the back of a vehicle. I hugged my wife and away she went off one way to get back in the car, and me in the other to go to war – again. Not begrudgingly, either. This was now truly my profession. My craft forever.

Echo Troop 2/11 gathered into formation and spent the evening drawing out weapons and equipment from the arm's room and then staged in a hall in the community center to wait for our busses to the airfield.

We arrived at SCLA, pronounced See-La, or Southern California Logistics Airport in Apple Valley near Victorville which is just down the road from Barstow on the way to Riverside and the Greater Los Angeles Basin. We boarded big beautiful airliners at sunrise with a light desert rain accompanying the desert sunrise. Rainbows were present. Next thing I know we were in Kuwait. We landed in the day-time because Kuwait was a secure place. Troop movements were much different than at 10th Mountain. We didn't stress as much. It was very grown-up and a bit odd to be honest. I had been with the 11th Armored Cavalry Regiment for 4 months now and all of it was different from before: From ever before at any time in my military experience up to this point. I really appreciated it in the moment and knew what a good thing it was and as this story moves about, I hope I can transmit to you this liberty at play in continuous military operations. This is not normal, but it wasn't wrong either. You were just expected to show up and go to work, and we did.

This is the land of Pazuzu. It used to be the Garden of Eden (so say the theologians). Then it was the birthplace of Algebra and the Algorithm and the Empty Ciphers of Baghdad and Babylon that held onto and improved mathematics. They did this with great help from India to the East - and hence why we call and classify our numbers as the Hindu-Arabic Numerals. Jupiter was tracked here by royal astron-omers leading to the world's first trigonometry tables. This ancient culture of two rivers preserved and improved the Greek School for a thousand years after Europe fell into the Dark Ages. But what about older things? Ancient stuff. Pazuzu is a demon that originates from the Mesopotamian Valley (The Tigris and the Euphrates) who it is said protects this land from, The Western Winds. Pazuzu is still on the job here. Does Pazuzu live in a car trunk in the modern day? Is that his vessel of choice? I have so many strange questions for and about Iraq and the Iraqi people themselves. Maybe not so much the people. I managed to spend enough time with them to know that they would just like the whole of the land to be quiet again. They really don't like us upfront, at face-value. Each new Westerner has to earn their faith with them one modern yard at a time.

Car trunk? Pazuzu? Western Winds? What is this crazy-talk?

The main body of Echo Troop had taken a ground convoy out of Kuwait up to Forward Operating Base Kalsu in Northern Babil Province, Babylon, Iraq. They had seen the Ziggurat at night by way of mention from our ever-observant and vigilant commander in the middle of one of their nights of travel. Overall, they arrived without incident. The rest of us got on a C-130 and flew at night to Al-Taqaddum airbase which is directly east of Baghdad and northwest of our designated operating area for the next 12 months. This is January of 2005. Our 12 months was end to end on a calendar year: January to December of 2005 - and was referred to operationally as Operation Iraqi Freedom III. It was here at Al-Taq as it was known in short that I woke up to my first morning in Iraq Proper. This was a transition point for us to re-assemble and take helicopters over to Kalsu.

Al-Taqaddum, as mentioned, is an Iraqi airbase. During combat operations, post-invasion, it served as an American airbase. It was here that you could take account, in-part, the assertion that during the invasion, no plane in the Iraqi air force managed to get into the air for more than 30 seconds - if at all. Most were taken out before they could ever be manned. As I strolled around our enclosures, interconnected by necessity, dividing areas in the same way, I noticed that each of the hard sites that were hangars for individual fighter planes had a single hole punched into the roof. It was here that an American aircraft or cruise-missile had found its target and turned the interior and all inside into plasma and junk. This reminded me of the ritual of virgin queen bees when a honeybee hive attempts to raise a new queen to replace the old one. The old queen and any newly hatched virgin queens that may have survived the initial birthing begin listening-for and seeking out "piping" queens. The sound that virgin queens make prior to hatching is called, "piping." If they don't get out in time, one of the queens will kill the hatching queen with one strike of the stinger through the cell-cap. That is what this is in terms of first-strike air-superiority in war.

Standing on the Al-Taq tarmac one evening in late January while waiting for our helicopter ride to Kalsu, there was a young African American NCO that was assigned to guiding our chalk (the contingent of Soldiers to be put on a bird). I was at a distance but I heard him talking about Fallujah and what had obviously impacted him by way of what had to have been the numerous comings and goings of forces in and out of the nearby city the month before. He wasn't soliciting alms or amplifying anything, he was giving his best straight word to those of us in line who were nearest to him. Soldiers counsel Soldiers just by talking to other Soldiers. When your language is universal, so too is the power of the enfranchised members. If I describe something to another Soldier, it is delivered in the Army syntax and the Army dialect and is instantly grasped. On paper it is called the Army Writing

Style, which conveys doctrine and its terms in first-person and with authority based on technical and tactical expertise which is more than privilege could ever muster.

We landed in the same place where we would get picked up a year from now, a large bed of stones laid out for helicopters. Another cobbled airfield. A makeshift landing zone destined for continual improvement. It was night and cold and clear. Deserts are the same no matter what during all phases of their yearly climate shifts. I guess all terrains share their own characteristics. Night in the desert is much more visceral and beautiful than during the day. It's almost as if this were a theater for the universe with showtimes from sundown to sun-up. Here it was a theater of war as well. Stars fell out of the sky in the form of flares, and mortar rounds, and rockets. There was no incident on the landing zone as we were herded off towards the Hesco walls nearest to us where a series of guides from the unit ground convoy and advanced party took ahold of us and began getting us sorted to our troop/company and platoon areas.

We woke up the next morning and we all found each other and started to figure out when and where chow was, where the command post was, what we were supposed to be doing. Our sector was manned by Marines and they would be the ones with whom we would conduct right seat/ left seat rides. A right seat/ left seat ride (RSLSR for brevity sake from here on out) is – again - when you accompany the leaders and units of the outgoing leaders and units so they can show you and your unit and your leaders the area of operations, the nature of the enemy, the characteristics you should expect in the performance of your men, weapons, and equipment in said-area, and to get the proverbial, "warm-fuzzy". The first patrol we went out on was a quick ride to see the towns of Haswah and Iskandiriyah. These were both to the northwest of Kalsu. I don't remember the patrol itself, but I remember meeting up on the hood of a Humvee with our commander and the Marine commander that would lead the RSLSR. Sometimes that is all there is in memory. I just remember it being cold and bright; and, hectic. And muddy.

Hectic. Remember the mention of us being big boys and moving about with a bit less formal rigidity? Well, with this comes the trade-off of "Hectic". You might be on the big boy program but you are expected to be working, and in the Army this is continuous. It's where "Busy Work" gets a bit of legitimacy because the definitive purpose of an Army is to hold ground like a Red Queen running in place.

Al-Haswah, or just Haswah, is a small busy city that is split into four quadrants with a road known to us as Route Jackson that split the place east, west. This was the y-axis. The north-south split that formed what is essentially the origin of a graph (the center of Haswah) was a combination of a road heading west to Iskandiriyah, known as Route Reba - and an estuary filled with stagnant water, sewage, and trash that went east. This was the x-axis. The patrol base was in the upper right (northeast) quadrant of this center crossing. +^. That's not the best symbolic representation because it was nestled directly into that L on the + where that carat (^) is. It was heavily fenced in with Hesco baskets as the initial foundation, machine gun bunkers on all of the high places, and only one gate in and out. There were apartments and businesses that curtained the north and east faces and they were rid-dled with bullet holes. Obviously there had been many confrontations over who owned the area. The west side was the small parking lot with Route Jackson and the gate paralleling. On the south was the estuary.

There were trails on both sides of the waterway and foot-traffic was continuous during the day.

Before we took over the operational control of the area we spent a good deal of time with our Marine counterparts. The Marines I met were wild. I never saw combat as a Marine but in this instance, I did not trust what I was seeing. This is not to say that the Marine Corps was deficient here, but they were definitely ready to go home. I was not impressed with how they would patrol and just randomly discharge their weapons to clear their paths. It was reckless. There was a SAW gunner of theirs that we chatted up. His take on this?

"Man, I killed so many people they took my weapon away from me for a while."

How much of this is true and how much is just shit-talking, I'll never know. Regardless, it was the reality and the impression before me. What was life like for them before us. Did it require this mode of aggression? Honestly, it probably did. Change is good. Fresh eyes are good. Watching one of the convoys tear up Route Jackson near the end of our time together, weapons ablaze, was answered with my questions of what the locals (and the insurgents thought): It was the first of a few incidents where one minute things were status-quo, and the next minute a casualty report was filtering back. Whether it was this vehicle or another, somewhere down that road they took their final casualties. One of their vehicles had been hit and there was no quorum on this whatsoever. It was just an event. Expected, if not earned. We now owned this inheritance of brutalism. My opinion of them is really just that. However, I trust the Marine Corps and I accepted and trusted the situation we now shared.

On our last RSLSR, we made a ground convoy between Haswah and Iskandiriyah to the west and we did this at night. Hectic tests systems. Hectic tests awareness. My vehicle was the trail vehicle and the Marines were in the lead. Not only are you driving fast but also keeping your distance. It's a fine bit of applied calculus to run ground attack convoys much as it is with any coordinated maneuvering of any form. There is a roundabout in Iskandiriyah where Route Reba branched off and took you back to Haswah that had a really large, golden teapot in the center. Now, at this point in time, I did not have my bearings on which turn-off it was back to Haswah and we had lost sight of the vehicle that we were trailing. Quick turns will do this. We circled around the teapot which would be with us as a notable urban terrain feature and I am certain must still be there today. We circled again. Hectic had been external up to now: Vehicle noises, air rushing by, radios crackling, gunfire intermittent but not relevant to us. But now, it was internalized. I ordered the vehicle to stop. There we were, in the middle of Iraq, beside a ludicrous-sized golden teapot as if a Djinn would come out and help us. We tried calling on the net and the handheld ICOM radios. Nothing. Just the Golden Teapot.

The answer to this was simple: We wait. There was nowhere to take cover without undermining what would be a return vehicle which I was certain would be our Marine convoy. My assumption was valid and after 2 or 3 minutes (which is a lifetime in this situation) they returned. After this, there were no more right seat, left seat rides with the Marines. We took charge of all positions and duties in sector and over the next few weeks we watched them withdraw in their convoys of amphibious tracks and Humvees and large trucks: 2 and 1/2 ton and 5 ton green monsters.

Haswah was our first concentrated effort as a troop. There were 3 line platoons and we rotated in and out of Haswah from the Forward Operating Base (Kalsu) which was southwest a few miles down Route Jackson and then around the way. Just as we rotated one platoon at a time into Haswah for duty in a 3-cycle, so too went operations inside Haswah. One squad took guard for 8 hours, one squad took patrols for 8 hours, and one squad was down for 8 hours. The guard consisted of towers and gate and command. Peering into the void. Doing nothing. Then you mounted vehicles for 8 hours and kept the roads open. What this means is, you got in your vehicles and if you weren't refueling or some other miscellany, you were driving down route after route just waiting to trigger an IED or have one triggered on you. It's very tiring and nerve-wracking and those two never make for a good mix.

We made foot patrols in addition-to and usually in conjunction with motorized patrols. One afternoon just north of the patrol base, an IED had been triggered that had been set into the concrete curb of the island that split the road as it attempted to become a highway of sorts leading out of the main cityscape and into the plains. I don't recall exactly how we came upon this incident, but it had blown the tires off of a Humvee belonging to the First Sergeant and the Troop Master Gunner. They were taking care of their own UXO (Unexploded Ordinance) report and waiting on Echo Troop Maintenance Platoon to come out with their M-88 Recovery Vehicle. Our maintenance sergeants ran the most squared-away motor pool in all of the war, I guarantee it. Echo Mechanics were Echo Soldiers first, last, and always and worked like professionals day and night for us - sharing every danger and always a pleasure to be around. Never gruff no matter how bad we abused their vehicles. Haha.

Our platoon sergeant (PSG) was out with our section (he rotated back and forth between the two maneuver sections that we had split the platoon into - along with the platoon leader) and he pointed me in the direction of the barber shop that was on the west side of the road. Apparently it had been hit with shrapnel. I walked over there with my squad and had them pull security. The PSG and I walked in and there was a shattered front barbershop window, a huge smear of blood on the floor, and a man who had been waiting to get his haircut with no head. The nonchalance was in here, too. It was just another day apparently. I don't remember the barber being in there. Obviously no-one else was getting trimmed on this day. Honestly, it's quite possible that someone else got a haircut later in the day. The Iraqi people were as strong as the Afghanis in the agoras. Life went on regardless. Business was business, bloodshed or not. One by one I drew my squad into the room so they could see a dead man and the effects of the weapon that killed him and the damage that a few slivers of weaponized steel and lead traveling at 13,000 mph can deliver. Then we retired back to Haswah about a mile back down Route Jackson.

Route Reba was a strange road. The second thing concerning Route Reba was one of several incidents where a vehicle had come too close to our forces and suffered the consequences. VBIEDS – Car Bombs were a big thing and very real. From nonchalance to hectic again. Like turning on a faucet. Not really a gushing faucet, either. Just enough to not be mistaken for Chinese water torture. I came upon one of our National Guard platoons from the 155th Mississippi Rifles to whom we were attached to that served as our BCT (brigade combat team) command in the hierarchy of units in Iraq during this phase of the war. The bodies of two men and one woman, all three Iraqi, were in the back of the pick-up truck they had died in. Did the Iraqi Police shoot them or did they run afoul of this convoy? Everyone was running around securing traffic and signaling vehicles and writing reports and transmitting reports. I stood next to the truck bed and looked at these three: Did they have a history? I mean, of course they did; but, was their history and the conduct of their lives worth us killing them? Were they just in a hurry to make ends meet for the day and forgot about the rule of staying 300 feet from U.S. forces, especially convoys? Nonchalance mixed with the pressing concerns of getting food or supplies or what have you could surely make one make such errors. This was the nature of war in this place. It was published, broadcasted, given ample bright signage; plenty of good decision-making and alibis were made by the young Americans behind these guns: We understood life and it took a very abrupt and forceful move on the part of a vehicle or person to pull a trigger here. Whatever the case, these three met a machine gunner and lost on a game of chicken, whether intentional or circumstantial it didn't matter. War is a calculus of measures. This was one of the more basic ones and would play out as the most common form of engagement right behind actually being attacked with bombs.

The first IED I went through was 2 IEDs. The first was too late and the second was too early. In this pocket was the reality of knowing you weren't dead in all of its existential form. The second indicator was a bit less philosophical and worrisome for half a second as my machine gunner who was up in the turret screamed like a little girl. Look, it happens. We all do it. At some point, there is a defined disconnect between our masculinity and our expressions in the face of horror. If you live and remain unscathed, it is never questioned. It is laughed at with a sophomoric reassurance of brotherhood; of boys dropping their defenses just long enough to say, "Wow, did you see/hear/feel that?" Every one of us in the vehicle grabbed the gunner and pulled him down and ran our hands all over him feeling for wounds or blood and asking him 35 times in 3.5 seconds if he had been hit; was he okay; and listening for, "I'm okay."

We were already gunning it down Route Jackson back towards Haswah but the gas pedal took on a whole new life and meaning. I'm pretty sure every right foot tried to backseat driver this moment as we sped on ahead just far enough to pull over and send up a UXO and general situation report. My radio work was calm and efficient voice-wise and thoughtful. Being the patrol leader, it was my duty to send up all information including the grid coordinates which I took with my little yellow Garmin that I coveted over the military equivalent, known as a PLGR ("Plugger"). I was adept in working my equipment without directly looking at it. This stems from generational tests of doing things like breaking down and reassembling weapons systems while blindfolded while under some form of duress. I began reading off all of the information other than the grid coordinates while I waited for the GPS to get its three satellites and spit out my alpha-numeric location. I did so in a very calm fashion. When it came time to read off the grid, I looked down at the screen and found my hand shaking. I had to reset and then read everything off my magic machine.

A final note on IEDs for the time-being: A single IED was usually at least 1 - 155mm artillery shell, but 2 or 3 was not uncommon. The explosion breaks the speed of sound. The chemicals composing the powder burn at 13,000 feet per second. This is initially trapped inside a steel casing that is more of an alien green ceramic that is thick and meaningful. These are not beer cans and they are not appliances. I don't remember the final weight of a single round, but if you have back trouble - you should not tackle one lightly in picking one up. In fact, you should probably get some help. Bundle these together and then blow one and you risk suffering brain damage being within what is called, "Danger Close". This distance is 400 meters for a 155 and is a general measure for judging where to place your rounds if you ever have to call them in on your own general vicinity. We went through two of these: Right between two of them. You almost wonder if a black hole opened up here because we were all generally okay. Just a bit, "shook" per-se.

Guard was less eventful each and every time we went on. The same stinky canal, the same chelubs barking in the night. The same chelubs staggering out and dying in the sun by day. Trash everywhere. It would be a great project to map trash patterns to pass time. You would never get bored. However that would be less-than-desired for the efforts of America's youth in war. We do range cards and we do beautiful and amazing works of art with each one. Even the simplest stick figures and scratches on paper by a Soldier attempting to convey his position and that which is in a visible (and invisible) arc in front of them is a demonstration that he or she cares about life. It is normally the duty of each position and each Soldier in that position to construct and update the range cards individually per their respective stations. We were quite fixed at the moment and this afforded me the opportunity to do three things: Make some really great range cards as an example for all, use one Soldier that was exceptional at art to do these, and to train my Soldiers by conveying my range card maker from one position to the next until all were up to snuff. The Soldiers standing guard could stand guard and the Soldier making the range cards could take guides from them and they in turn could see a demonstration of what right looks like – through one of their own. For me or another rank to do it is expected. When you push the training down between your best and brightest in each category (in this case art – drawing), you get a better listening and learning audience.

We also sent out patrols through the small city at night. Not attacks. Just presence patrols. The presence patrol is standard first-order policing in civics. The military (any military) establishes the first governments in combat and our systems bridge the effects of war and the hand-off to the civilian apparatus and their elected officials over time as security and resources improve. Nation-building. However, even with the hip name and its criticisms, COIN (counterinsurgency) and nation-building are old as dirt and not going away and we have a responsibility to perfect and steward military operations other than war with dignity and perseverance back towards agreeable order for all. Simple, unique demonstrations - with stuff never used before and maybe only seen in a book, video (this is all before YouTube mind you), or film is always best for Soldiers: A practical example: There was an old car that had been a VBIED (Vehicle-Borne Improvised Explosive Device) just sitting in the middle of an open area of the town where city-planners from different eras probably took a handoff of everything except each other's ideas and left a place where a roundabout probably could have gone – but was probably more useful as a market square or plaza. I had a thermite grenade that is designed to cut steel and burns at 4000 degrees to make this possible. Good for melting an engine block. I let everyone know the plan and we watched the car burn in the night – for a second time. A twice-baked potato. On the final push back to the patrol base, I found a small puppy rummaging through a garbage pile. I named her Maxine. This was before there was a ban on dogs. Having a unit dog was pretty common. Maxine was instantly loved. She ran around all inside the patrol base at Haswah and my wife had enthusiastically sent Maxine her own collar with dog tag; her own bowl and treats; and, I don't know what else but Maxine was pretty set after that.

The Hateen Weapons Factory – before we destroyed it – was the largest munitions production facility in the world. The Insurgents – the predecessors of ISIS who were seeking to take full advantage of the power vacuum to establish a myriad of micro-regimes – would hold kangaroo courts here. Dead judgements with their faces cut off and left to rot. What was left here? What was hiding here? Nothing really the day we came. My squad was in the Army Times Photos of the Year for 2005 however – running up a berm. We were not posing – but we were also not in much danger. This was one of the last patrols I remember before we began opening up the farmlands to the direct east.

Changing out units at the patrol bases was usually done under the cover of darkness for obvious reasons. Doesn't mean you won't get attacked and it doesn't mean that spies won't take count or get an accurate count at that. However, it is just best-business-practices to do so. Speeding down Route Jackson I heard both a 25mm and a 240 Bravo (7.62mm) erupt followed by vehicles stopping. There is a curfew. Anyone out will be shot, no questions asked (usually); especially if those people are standing on the side of the road like an IED trigger team. There is no reason to be out in those fields on the side of the road in the middle of the night except under conditions of freedom – and this was a place of anything but at that time. In a Muslim country just like the darkened village of Mangretay in Afghanistan – Muslims do Muslim practices and that is defined at night by being indoors, together, in the company of their loved ones, and enjoying the essence of life as they understand it to be in their hearts – not checking the farm on the side of the road.

There was only one man that we found, dead. It is most likely the other two either escaped or died of wounds deep in the reeds. He was a big guy. He was shot center mass - as we are experts and professionals at this exact trade. He was floating in the water that irrigated the field and one of us would have to jump in and pull him out. No-one was joking but we were particularly petty at this particular juncture because we were coming out fresh and new to the wire. We were all clean, in fresh clean uniforms, and did I mention clean? Here we were, United States Riflemen. We know all of the grit and passion of the soil and we worship it in many aspects. However, not that night. Finally the platoon sergeant had to make a bargain: Whomever jumped in and pulled him out could return to Kalsu for the night to shower up and come back out the next morning. I'm not one to pass up free chicken. I was now confident my squad could be run by my senior team leader for a few hours at least so I jumped in and pulled him out. He was a big guy. Dead people already weigh a lot. Everything is heavier when wet.

April. Alpha Troop – one our tank companies - had routinely but softly patrolled in Diyarah up to this point. Their duties were often fixed on highway security on Route Tampa and all of the overpasses and the on- and off-ramps. The road leading to Diyarah needed all of the watching it could get. Maybe it was just pushes down Cleveland and some initial HUMMWV patrols. Word was that we were going to open up a new patrol base in this small and offset farming community which lay to the northeast of FOB Kalsu, across the main state route – which is/was Tampa. Haswah and Iskandiriyah were all towns, economies:

Agoras in strife. Markets in a state of cannibalism. Diyarah was the same, but smaller. There was just enough development and capital influence in Diyarah to interrogate it and the surrounding farmlands for bomb-makers. There was extensive crime family in this region. Not sure how they are doing today.

I brought my squad out one morning on a first patrol down Route Cleveland and the Diyarah Proper areas. I decided about half-way down the three mile stretch to get out and just walk about half a mile. The mornings were very green and pink and beautiful. The farms peaceful. The walk was uneventful as the drivers followed closely. This is not Baghdad. The other nearby towns were also not Baghdad. Dangerous and confining yes, but not the deadly and vast labyrinth of civic infrastructure. You feel okay out here because as an Infantryman this is your real ecosystem: Nature. The high-wall-scapes of the city find a below-the-horizon equivalent here: Farms need water and water comes by way of canals – usually. It most certainly does in Iraq when you are nestled between the Tigris and Euphrates. The labyrinth changes form as it extends beyond congested civilization. You can't just hop a canal in a Bradley or Humvee and most times you can't do it on foot. You could be standing right across from where you have to go and then have to go as much as an hour or two around just to get there. This alludes to the tactical leader that route planning and mission objectives had to be finite and determined in advance for risk of these trapping effects. However, Google Earth had been around since 2001 and it was rapidly becoming our goto even as major portions of our operational map were being blotted out due to the fact that any update could show our positions. That's how powerful we are. We shut down a public good, in part, to protect our strategy and our lives. Go look at Paris or something. However, as an Infantry leader you still get disappointed when a resource like this is down even if the reason is for your own protection. A paradox for sure.

Our first KIA was from first platoon. I did not know the young man but his friends obviously did. I had received the word of his death from my platoon sergeant and as I left my tent to go find my own squad and do whatever it is we had to do for the day I headed down the row of tents and the concrete walls that partitioned off our areas safely to contain the blasts of enemy mortars that may fall at any given time. The idea being that these pockets would absorb the munitions and keep casualties to a minimum. As I got closer to first platoon's tents it became much more real. Your friends are all you have here. You can say there are commanders and plans and rules and regulations and that the mission is what you're all about but it is the ancient maxim of esprit-de-corps (Latin for "the spirit of a unit") that prevails and this is generated from the individual Soldier. Each brings their own part of the United States that they hail from and all of the talents and quirks they may possess. We have at our disposal a rich fellowship of experience and ideas and differences that help each new generation appreciate why service to country is so important and how we all truly hope the rest of life plays out well when we return to our original status as Citizens. When I opened the tent flap all I saw was this wicked Baroque-like painting: You know, the ones where all of the action in the painting is wild and bursting with energy. The underwater lensing like there is a jazz lounge at the bottom of a swimming pool. These men were angry and the one's who had been on patrol were now mixed in with the one's who were on their down time and well, now everyone was putting on their gear hot for something to do to answer for the loss of their friend. Someone had to pay in their minds. Perfectly rational in war. On a small canal road on the north end of the farms that we now took control of as our area of operations was an IED packed beneath the caked Mesopotamian mud. His friends loved him very much and as I closed the flap and consoled the one man who had taken a moment to step outside sweating and crying – I was at a loss on what to say or do other than put my hands on his shoulder. Nothing much you can do at this point other than be there and listen and make time stand still.

The morning of April 28th began with waking up in the back of one of my Bradleys. We had spent the night as the traffic control point on Route Cleveland about half of a mile up from the new patrol base. You lay out wire, markers, scorpion tails, etc; and then - integrate them with your vehicles and heavier weapons pointing wherever necessary. Technically you should have a range card built for this, too. Two of them. Usually up and down the road. My first squad leader in the Army, from whom I gathered many fine first and last lessons, never took part in watch when on patrol. We would go to ground somewhere in the forests of Drum and he would put out what time he needed to be up and then went straight to sleep. No-one even thought of questioning it and he would induce self-organizing behavior as the team leaders, real or assumed, went about establishing shifts. This of course is not the same from leader to leader and derives definitively from competency. Squad leaders run the Army. Team leader may be the hardest job, but squad leaders move everything and are the only billet in the Army that is both in the noncommissioned officer support channel and the chain of command. It's a great moment in time when you get a squad, especially in combat. I had managed to establish myself firmly enough upon arrival at the National Training Center the preceding August to simply say, "wake me up at _____" and "do this or that". It is at this special equilibrium where this directness takes on an unassuming and disarming appeal to the listeners. This takes a little practice and earnest effort to integrate doctrine with professional faith in others but in no other institution in the world will you get so many opportunities to learn the craft of real leadership. Philosophy surely stopped that evening when I said, "I will see you guys in the morning. Don't kill us." The rest is a trusted application.

During this time we began undergoing a change of command at the troop (company) level. Our incoming and outgoing commanders were conducting their right-seat, left-seat rides (RSLSR again). They had to travel many times between all of the company areas doing inventory and orienting the terrain for the new commander and allowing the outgoing (or current) commander to make final suggestions and recommendations to his or her relief. They had come through during the night and were pleased with the TCP and my men and that is all you need for a good day in the Army. "Mission first, men always" will always get you on the right foot at a glance.

When I arrived from 10th Mountain I was in top-shape, and top-form. Never before and never again was I exactly what I was intended to be as a professional Soldier. It was the tip of Maslowe's hierarchy of needs: The self-actualization. Our unit had been locked into its traditional role at the National Training Center as the OPFOR – or, Opposition Force. Here in the middle of the Mojave just outside of Barstow is where the Army sends its brigade combat teams to work on its operational architecture and get their bells and whistles up before combat. NTC – along with the Joint Readiness Training Center in Louisiana – is a part of most unit life-cycles regardless of whether the nation is at war or not. Most of the people in our unit were not up to speed on basic infantry drilling as traditional riflemen because of this: However, the Army saw it clear to send a bunch of Soldiers and NCOs from the major line units that had been in the opening stages of Afghanistan and the Invasion of Iraq. A lot of talent poured in from everywhere and it was everywhere apparent as we dug in the last four months before coming to Iraq.

In my particular lane, I was given almost free-reign to shape my squad and in-turn, for a moment, the platoon. All of my luck and fortune came through as we started from basic walking, crawling, and weapons-handling to breaching wire, entering and clearing a trench both day and night, and finally a full table of vehicles and men converging on a platoon objective as a culminating exercise. I did so good (I'll stop soon I promise haha) that my platoon leader had to stop my commander from giving me more awards. It was so congenial and wonderfully satisfying to do everything I was supposed to do in one fell swoop and have somebody see it that has some actual say in your fate. Things sway like this that easy in an Army, good and bad. From here on out I was trusted uniquely, and more-so than ever-before, and I really love that moment and my commander for it. Our higher commander – our squadron commander had a single philosophy for his young officers that I learned about later, "Ensure your systems are in place." My systems were in place. That is such a great feeling, too.

He and the incoming commander died near where our traffic control point had been set up the night before. Our new patrol base was a straight shot down Route Cleveland. A vehicle was coming towards the patrol base as the incoming and outgoing commander saddled up in a stripped-down convoy where there were just two vehicles and minimal personnel (driver, gunner, commander in each). Everyone was on their missions and we were becoming adept in fast movements between points to conserve combat power being stripped away. I don't know exactly how many captains (O-3 rank in the Army) or what percentage of the total deaths captains made up for the Iraq War – but it was a lot. Captains did mad work in this war. This was a counterinsurgency after the Invasion. Guerilla warfare. However, Armies don't traditionally "go native" and we do it for the sake of establishing order. We are never seen at-ease. We don't put on different clothes at night. We don't go home until we go all of the way home – however that turns out. After the fighting or as the fighting is worked towards a conclusion, the image of a uniform and stable presence is philosophically supposed to induce stability through a positive and readily identifiable security posture which tells the casual observer that there is some semblance of law and that progress can begin again and new enterprises can be joined in safety. Where formations and arrays of equipment usually do this – here it is the appearance and conduct of the individual Leaders and Soldiers on the battlefield in small cameos demonstrating how well our Country and its Army prepares even the lowest ranking man for leadership in war. With Captains and Sergeants this is always the standard – but because it is the standard it rarely stands out. Again, formations usually make bland the vast talent our ranks possess as they work for the unit and mission.

Leadership by example is played out from age-to-age. It is getting harder to come by, too. Most convoys would have had a few Soldiers in seats to take care of these vehicle searches and any other tactical situations that may arise, however on this day the only two people who were readily available without dropping a crucial part of the already stretched task-organization were the two captains. The vehicle probably seemed harmless as all war is based on the deceiving of one's enemy. Up to this point, we had searched thousands of cars and thousands of times neither I (expecting to do so) or my friends had run into such misfortune. The two commanders died at the back of this vehicle to an IED mounted inside its trunk. In doing so they saved the lives of many Soldiers just down the road to where it had been heading. In an instant we lost both our incoming and outgoing commanders and seeing the "for who" part of a radio transmission requesting body bags sent us all racing to consolidate and reorganize.

Our squadron commander recommended both of his captains for Silver Stars. Both were denied. The tragedy of the awards system is for someone else to sort through but as of the time of this writing, SFC Alwyn Cashe still has not received posthumously the Medal of Honor that we all feel he deserves. Though Cashe was not part of our unit, he was in country the same time as we were and his story covers anything I would have to say in a better way. An example of the future consequences of such a broken awards system is that Cashe's son who is currently in the Army, if he had been qualified in all standard ways, he would have been given a direct nomination (without a congressional nod) to any service academy of his choice because of his father's heroism. How many of these stories are lost under blanket administration?

That afternoon our entire troop was pulled off of the line and Alpha and their tanks came back to Diyarah as we filtered back into Kalsu to deal with the shock and re-constitute (with a new commander) afterwards so we could continue operations. Killing a commander is one of the pinnacle successes for a combatant in war. It does horrifying things to the morale and discipline of a unit. Killing two is almost unheard of.

Selfishly I thought about the traffic control point the day before and the promise of the reputation of my hard work being passed onto the next guy shattered as they were both dead. Stories and information in general are of the highest valued currencies because they portray a situational and tangible picture and can help offset a bad first impression; and, deter the nuisance of reinventing the wheel. However, their memory was rooted in duty. Simple duty that held no outwardly apparent glory for either men: Just another car and probably nothing. They did their duty simply and with no fanfare and the two men who grew up together, went to West Point together, commanded companies in combat together (the other captain had been the headquarters company commander and was next fulfilling his requirements for command on the line), died together. They are buried a few feet apart in the West Point Cemetery. My commander and his friend are the only graves I have visited since the end of my time in combat.

May has a few remarkable things in my memory. We began fighting with higher-ups about a policy of driving 25 mph "to look for IEDs." We used to joke that we would tie the most junior man in each vehicle to the front and whenever they started squirming we would know there was a bomb. Obviously just a joke, but by the darkness of that humor you can rest assured it was not a joke to us. In a CBRN (Chemical, Biological, Radiological, Nuclear) environment, the lowest ranking man is to discard the safety of his or her equipment and expose themselves for the sake of others. Like the canary in the coal mines it is to be accepted. Our last KIA and wounded happened at a small bridge that spanned the canal cutting route Cleveland. An EFP

– Explosive-Formed Penetrator – had been strapped to the bridge. As their convoy passed, the EFP was detonated by a trip wire across the road, killing the young sergeant and taking the arm of another. I ran into our wounded man a few years later as he was participating in one of the DC parades with the Purple Heart Association. Today he teaches instrumentation to naval aviators. On some of the final patrols with our original platoon I remember two things regarding the Iraqi Police: Coming up on a traffic control point on the Haswah side of Cleveland where an Iraqi Policeman (IP) had been shot in the head during an attack that had only happened a few minutes before; his brains in a neat wet pink pile on the black asphalt of the rainy ground on an overcast spring day. Grey, black, red, pink, green all around. The next was when we went to visit the Iraqi police station on Route Reba between Haswah and Iskan. It's against Islam to drink alcohol and let me just say, I think that's a superior philosophy for Islam because my practicing Muslim Iraqi policemen were drunk as hell and flashing their usually friendly and peaceful eyes in very sinister ways. They did this inbetween haranguing the prisoners who were all locked up together in big bunches waiting on bail which is really just extortion of the families. I don't want to bring up Shaytan again but the Devil shone bright in those men's eyes. More so than I have ever seen in any other drunk. On the way back to wherever we were going to sleep that night our convoy got hit with an IED within a few hundred meters of the station. Fortunately it only blew out a tire which we rapidly fixed. Whomever fired it must have been drunk.

I don't exactly remember when "The Hen" arrived to my squad to become my new team leader as one of my others had gone off to the sniper section. I was instantly impressed and would come to be as

grateful as any leader for a subordinate leader who was always looking to get to me for the fresh word and to get the work done: He was
passionate, sensible, and super experienced by now as he had done the
Invasion, been extended in theater to OIF II (Operation Iraqi Freedom
II – OIF I (One) was the Invasion), and after returning briefly stateside
and requesting duty at Fort Irwin like the rest of us – found himself
right back in Iraq for OIF III. The Hen gets his name from one of the
first times I came to check on him in his own living space. I found him
sitting criss-cross applesauce on his cot, showered and in shorts with
a perfectly clean white cotton crew neck sweater. I called him Mother
Hen as the rest of the troops around him were struggling immediately
to get on his level. For the sake of brevity I'll just call him Hen.

The Hen had been on the CSM's (Command Sergeant Major's)
PSD – Personal Security Detachment. He had fallen out of favor with
the CSM and ended up back on the line and in my squad. He told
me upfront that he was glad as hell to be away from all of that and it
reflected immediately. I had a young, eager expert and professional
non-commissioned officer ready to work for me and that is gold. Gold
I tell you. The Hen did everything right. His gear was always squared-
away, his courtesy to his own troops was remarkable. I like to think
I'm pretty good at that: I was amateur to this man in his sincerity and
demeanor to his own men even when disciplining them. This showed
through as well even during corrective training. The Hen – not very
happy with his fire-team one day – a day off no less – had his men
construct from scratch a proper fighting position.

A proper fighting position is six feet deep, two feet chest to back
and two rifles wide. A proper fighting position has overhead cover (a
roof). A proper fighting position has a parapet where grenades (along

with sumps) work to keep the harmful effects of grenades away from you. A proper fighting position has aiming stakes and a range card – or two. A proper fighting position is a pain in the ass to build. His men built it and in broad daylight in front of the command tents and not one complaint – but an abundant amount of admiration by everyone else. The Hen was so amazing.

There is one other reason I love the Hen. One day we were chasing a bad situation in a farm and an Apache on station was guiding us to a house. When we got to the house I stood there and there was a door open. It was black beyond. No sign. My platoon sergeant had someone else off to the side but I was ascertaining going through this door. I just stood there. It was the only indecisive moment I had in war. I think the Hen saw this because he walked right past me and into the house. It is generally not my place to go in first, but I wasn't saying anything either. It was just a weird time and space but I'm glad it was just that. The Hen lives in my heart.

June brought with it heavy recruiting of the more experienced sergeants in the troop by my platoon leader who was being assigned to lead a MiTT or Military Transition Team which would detach itself from the troop and form as its own command under the current battalion structure in sector. There was already a dedicated MiTT for the forming of the Iraqi Army in our area and we would take these men who were coming out of their formation stage and take them on their first combat patrols. I was reluctant but then I realized that this was a good primer for Special Forces if I ever decided to attend Selection (which I didn't). This was a real opportunity to work in even more autonomy, more responsibility, and ultimately a positive international effect on the people of Iraq through their Soldiers. We gathered one afternoon to head over to the Iskan Army Base where we would set up our quarters inside the old hospital next to the power plant along the Euphrates. Our MiTT platoon was commanded by a first lieutenant and divided into four sub-elements: Three 4-5 man sections composed of a staff sergeant and three juniors plus a medic. Just like an ODA (A-Team) but not. I don't like these comparisons much but it is important to stress how important and influential unconventional warfare was - broad-based for us in this unconventional war and that because it takes so long to produce a Special Forces Soldier, their lessons had to be pushed down and exercised routinely throughout joint operating forces in both theaters. Storytelling, mission summaries, the poetics: All of these pass on the lessons unseen and unheard of with each new bard. You envision what you might do by these and if and when these moments do come: You make your first few broad brush strokes with legends, myths, and heresy. The inspiration and building blocks are open-source. The refinement is on you.

We loaded up our bags into our three Humvees, received a patrol brief which was standard anytime you left the wire, and headed out. Now, I will mention Killer Cam because Killer Cam is a true blood. Cam was born in Mexico and he used to tell of his days in Mexico selling Chiclets to make money for his family wearing a bright colored woven poncho. But more, Cam is a friend and I personally have never met a person that had any grievances with him. Cam drove this day and we were super happy for some reason. It was like going off to camp or something. It was campy. Like we could be blown up in any moment between here and Iskan but the sun was hot, the sky was blue, and there was the spirit of a unit looking to do good things with the Iraqi Army. We genuinely felt this way. In honor of our inspiration of

A-Teams we called ourselves Operational Detachment Echo (which was our troop designator, "E") and it was recognized as that under the callsign, "Thundercats." All around that is encouraging to be creators when your primary occupation is as destroyers. We were going to train new killers, but we were going to take great care and our enthusiasm was from the heart of good. Good fighting men are a blessing to any society. We were laughing and joking loudly as we turned onto Route Jackson to head north towards the left turn at Haswah taking us over to Iskandiriyah by way of Route Reba. The asphalt was fresh and black and shiny and had the wet look. It was beautiful under the Mesopotamian sun. Our laughing halted when we zoomed past a small puppy weeping over its sibling struck in the middle of road by some vehicle forever ahead of us. Maxine was getting bigger now and she was with us and would she would make her home wherever I was; wherever we were. Cam is very sensitive even to this day about the people in his life and he was quick to talk about how messed up the world was and I know he did this to set us all at ease just because it's a duty between us. It's that instant. We just immediately start caring for each other moment after moment. It's pretty awesome.

You get to the Golden Teapot and head south. To the right are massive power grid boxes and power line arrays where the nearby hydroelectric plant traded its river energy with 1/3 of the Iraq population. To the left is a wide-open marsh with reeds and a train track cutting across north-south. I would see one train run its course the entire time left. I think I stopped the convoy just to watch it. The Iskan Army Base was co-located with the hydroelectric plant - with its four massive smoke stacks and main plant seated alongside the east side of the Euphrates River. The camp itself had a parade ground where all good things in an Army happen. My first sight of our troops was them in formation struggling with indifference and the final tutelage of their basic training instructors who were other sergeants from our squadron. The sun was bright as I said but now it was dusty as the formations massed, moved, and kicked up dust. We immediately started tracking down Iraqi officers and orienting them to our presence. Our billeting was arranged to be in the old hospital. We downloaded all of our gear and likewise found the main American MiTT commander for our squadron to round out our assumption of command and duties. It's process about 12 or 13 steps long. There was a flagpole on the parade ground at the south end atop which the Iraqi national colors flew. It was a proud thing.

The first order of business was to play Simon Says. Interpreters were always under duress of being sold out and-or unreliable. Many days you would be without. I figured what better way to bridge any future deficit in this regard than to begin a rapport based on charades and this can be certainly founded in Simon Says. I had the platoon sit and suggested they follow my hand movements. They did. They sat there, criss-cross applesauce – rifles across their laps and patted their heads in unison with me. From here on out I added great gesticulation, parodic forms, hand-gestures, and loud audible sound effects to each and every period of instruction and wherever and whenever tactically sound.

Next was PCC/PCI. Pre-Combat Checks and Pre-Combat Inspections. PCCs are where you tie down your equipment properly and make sure all of it is in its correct places and checking to make sure it all fits snug against a few hard bumps and crawls. You have to shake yourself down. PCIs are where you inspect the outcome and is usually done by the maneuver commander of the unit being inspected. The best one of these inspections is the tie downs for the canteens. You make a nice end of the line bowline and do some square knots, here and there, with the 550 cord. Then you take your Bic lighter, burn them down at the ends to make small hammer heads so your ends won't pull back through. You make these hammer heads by placing the metal flame protector of the lighter against a bulb of hot black liquid nylon that stays like this just long enough to impress and flatten: Your cord will not slip back through. You do this for everything you carry. It gets pretty crazy once you start stacking systems and fine-tuning things like 550 cord hooks on the bottom of magazines for magazine changes. For the purpose of our Iraqis, a general issue of traditional load-bearing equipment or LCE with two canteens with pouches was the order of the day.

The canteen tie-down also afforded the best charade slash pantomime slash absurd parody. I found one of my Iraqi Soldiers without a tie down around his canteen and what caught my attention was the flap was unbuttoned. I walked up behind him, snatched it out, and threw it hard over my shoulder. This of course disrupts everything and it is here under the searing sun where for thousands of years, Armies have raged across these very lands beneath my feet and many have most certainly perished from losing their equipment at inopportune times or succumbing to dehydration and death from a lack of water under the horrible rigors of maneuver warfare – AND – that it is very import-ant that we keep our equipment – especially our canteens collectively secured to our persons. This was further exemplified as I scratched at the Earth on my knees, gurgling loudly, and flailing about until they all laughed and I finally mocked a death by loss of canteen. With all of this and a few other exercises including running to and from their flagpole so they got the basic idea down, we began patrolling.

I don't remember the first patrol but I do remember the first impression of the troops I now trained and led in combat. My Iraqis were all about the command of execution. If you pointed your finger they would barely ask a question other than to begin steadfast in pointed-direction. Our company was out in their Bongo trucks – the big Bongos – not the little utility trucks. Someone yelled for everyone off the trucks and they appeared like Djinn suddenly down from the bed of their trucks four feet off the ground to a semi-ready security posture on the side of the road. When you tell us Americans to do shit you will hear every motherfucker on that truck tell you about getting off. God Bless America but for sure God Bless obedient troops! There is really few things above this requirement for a half-way decent army. There has to be instant willingness and obedience to orders and teamwork – discipline. The most profound of these commands for us in this day was concerning our arch-nemesis: The Bomb. The IED. To the Arabic-speaking Iraqi Soldier: Boombala. And Boombala was planted by Ali Baba.

Ali Baba and the Forty Thieves. Ali Baba was the good guy in the story from the 1001 Arabian Nights. However in this story – it is intended as derogatory to the enemies of Iraq. The Insurgents, the al-Qaeda operators, and a host of other factional sorts that plotted our deaths daily were all Ali Baba. Ali Baba is universally understood in Iraq War terminology and with the Iraq People as the enemy. I caught this right away and had many sidebars on patrol with my Iraqis when an interpreter was near that Ali Baba was actually the good guy in the stories. Not too sure they had read that story.

Back to pointing. Saying "Ali Baba" or "Boombala" if a suspected IED was the case - was as magic as "Open Sesame." Their disregard for their own personal safety to have a chance at glory was all I needed to know I was okay with these men. Yes of course they could turn on you. Yes, some have unfortunately in other chapters of the war. But, with us – we had no such troubles. This could go either direction but our Iraqis were all from the same town in Iraq so it wasn't like the real Army where you went home and no one else was there except maybe one or two others. For them, their lore was built together and would return home with them – all together back to the same hometown. They truly had to fight for each other for the sake of personal honor and reputation in the long run without recourse. Very beneficial for us as their trainers and first operational combat leaders. Honor is best brought out from within in each new relationship and they already had theirs wired pretty tight.

This enthusiasm however bled over into fire discipline and we had to be very hands-on (not heavy-handed) or they would either shoot themselves in the foot or one of their own if we didn't grab their attention and their barrels on occasion while simultaneously conducting real combat operations in sector. The threat of them leading themselves into each other and getting one of us shot while we shepherded them through both the routine and the rigorous was a real fear. One night we sent a platoon out of Diyarah down Cleveland to check out a possible IED planted on the side of the road. All we saw was the vehicle stop, a loud shouting, and then a mad minute on the right side of the road. Muzzle flashes in the dark. They were keen on getting Ali Baba.

An air assault is a combat operation where you utilize helicopters to get to your objective and - in most cases – to return to your station of origin. We are very proficient as an Army with the use of the air assault that goes all the way back to the Korean War when helicopters made their first debut in war. This one machine's importance in modern war is never to be undercut when it comes to its dynamism as both a lifesaver in the mode of air transportation and a life-taker in the close-air support mode. We conducted a night air assault on a farm north of Diyarah. Before take-off we went through our operations order, sand table, and glasshouse rehearsals. There was to be an F-18 on station providing illumination on the target house. I had never seen this before and was expecting some half-ass pointer that no-one could see. Not sure why my faith was limited at the moment but after the commotion of getting my Iraqis off the helicopter into the field, going from man to man and setting him into a hasty defensive posture before moving out, I took my own moment to get myself right and set my monocular back down and swept the landscape to look for my target house. From an F-18 at 20,000 feet which I could not see or hear was this massive cone of infrared light that shone down from a clear starry night as if God had a flashlight right onto the house. Nothing had ever been clearer in a night operation than this – ever. More, to know that this plane could hold this exact beam while flying high above really re-inspired me on the go. How freaking awesome is it to have that kind of help? I feel safe.

The rest of the night was as I stated earlier, a quest to get our work done without shooting each other. Besides a few scares, the Iraqi men did a fine job. We spent the rest of the night pushing south and conducting sensitive sight exploitations (basically just making sure all bases were covered in regards to information gathering). We moved to daylight and at BMNT (Before Morning Nautical Twilight) artillery parachute flares were called in. The eyes need extra help during the twilights of before morning and end of evening (which really means dusk). The casings whip through the air and whistle and flap and all of the rest and the shadows of the palm trees in massive groves we happened to be standing in danced everywhere like some lost chapter of the Arabian Nights. Not explosive rounds – rounds to see by. Phosphorous dangling from little parachutes shot from 10 miles away so we could see just a little better and put artificial Djinn in the minds of anyone who might mean us harm.

We did a lot of patrols. A lot of hot hikes through the farms and a lot of courtesy patrols many times a day through Diyarah and to visit locals. One day we heard an explosion out in one of the fields. It was a ways off and we pretty much resigned it to being an IED on Tampa. Reports eventually filtered back that it had been a bomb-maker trying out one of his own products on himself.

Our commander had to mentor and develop the Iraqi company commander, Captain Majid. I was the senior enlisted man of our MiTT after the first "First Sergeant" had completed his duty. So, my pseudo-role as First Sergeant, or better – as Thundercat 7, I accompanied the commander in almost all other things except when I had my own platoon to train and lead. We had a lot of responsibility and we went about it merrily and with steadfast assurance. It was unsettling to the Iraqi officers the kind of non-chalance and irreverence we are allowed to openly display with and towards our own officers. Iraqi officers are very caste oriented and enlisted men are one step above dogs to them.

We started off operations with our Iraqi company at the Haswah patrol base and nudged our way over to Diyarah about 6 miles east. The first couple get-togethers with Majid were at Haswah in what was most certainly a family room or dining room at one point in time. I don't even remember what the building was originally. Officers mentoring officers in front of enlisted men is not a common occurrence and as I mentioned – most certainly not an Iraqi Army thing. Majid was noticeably uncomfortable as I looked on no matter how disarmed and casual I tried to be to reassure him that it wasn't personal. I did however have to hold back my smiles on occasion as my commander was a very good leader and he taught the right thing always (mostly through personal example – but also in sound doctrinal and philosophical counsel and orders) and hearing even the most constructive criticism outloud from a foreign officer was almost really more than he could bare.

There was a breakthrough about four mentor-sessions in where Majid was getting resources coordinated more effectively and in our war as with any war since the introduction of the combustion engine – oil and gas products are of crucial importance: Everything from the machines you ride on, to the ones that keep you warm, to generating electricity when a generator can be acquired. War for oil indeed. I believe in technological progress and green energy must be developed, but oil is forever – too. Just like the sunshine (or stars in general), the air, the plants – so too the oil and gas. You have to secure oil and gas simply because if someone else has it and they know nothing else about what to do with it – will set everything on fire with it out of ignorance. It's a regulated commodity for sure.

A pseudo-example of this could be found at the gate to Haswah in the opening months of our deployment where I would take an oil pan and fill it with sand, soak it in gas, and then light the sand-fuel mixture. This was for when it was cold to provide a bit of warmth and fascination. More fascination than warmth. Now in summer it was all fascination. Harmless, controlled, but in competent hands as well. The rest is not so with the world. You only had to look outward from that very gate into the town and see that most of civilization is in a state of disrepair with hulks and spillage and rot everywhere. All of it kind of begging to be set on fire because the pains of moving it or the complexity of engineering new stuff from it or recycling at the very least is all too complex for folks whose only crime in most cases is simply being poor. What our commander was teaching Majid was that supply chain management and supply economy determined his unit's effectiveness in combat; that improving the systems improved the world around him and this made for a more righteous army. The more righteous army wins not only on the battlefield, but after the wars the Soldiers are better people than when they arrived because of the liberal nature of adapting reason, science, and technology to the art of war. It brings us closer to finding resolution to conflicts faster and stabilizing regions much quicker so life can commute productively again.

Big Bongo trucks. Just big trucks with big beds and metal overhead frames for a covering which was never used in summer. I don't remember seeing any in winter either. These were packed with the platoons of our Iraqi company as we would transport them back and forth. One platoon would be at Diyarah, one would be off, and one would be training. Back and forth between Diyarah and Iskandiriyah – up and down Route Cleveland. When you reach the Main State Route (MSR) it is like any other highway in America: There are spiraling onramps and offramps that curve around at a reasonable grade of incline to bring vehicles sensibly on and off the highway. We were heading back to Iskan one afternoon and my vehicle was trailing the Bongos jam packed with one of the platoon's men. The vehicle was speeding up as we began to reach the MSR. It should have been slowing down to meet the necessary turn. We could barely get a radio transmission out before we saw the lead Bongo miss the turn to the onramp and disappear over the edge.

There is no way that ended well. Everyone was either saying this or thinking this. We raced up to the edge expecting to see a truck spilled on its side and its cargo of 30 humans smashed out all around. Nope. There they were, upright – still driving, everyone seated, looking for a way back onto the road. Literally just driving in circles inside the bowl created by the onramp and the overpass. Unbelievable. How the hell they remained intact is just beyond me. We just sort of looked around like kids to see if anyone else saw and then drove the rest of the way back to the Euphrates. Again: That Bongo drove straight off a virtual cliff with 30 men and nothing happened. They just kept on driving, not a man scratched.

Then I went on Block Leave. It was the end of September – beginning of October. It was finally my turn to take a break. I didn't take leave in Afghanistan in the regular way and here I was going to just get up and return home to Barstow from Iraq like a commercial break between a television program. It takes a while to transit out of country and get back to Kuwait. Once you get there you kind of sit around a bit more and then fly out. My airplane landed in Dallas and in the course of getting off to change planes and head on to Ontario, California, we were all immediately mobbed with so much cheering and enthusiasm and love that it was simultaneously a sense of immense pride and joy and an unsettling realization that all of these people had taken time out of their lives to come here and give us hugs and gifts and talk to us and pat us on the back and make us feel wanted. I don't care what the politics are, that experience of our homecomings in these airports was so wonderful. We really felt loved. If you were ever one of those people who came out to welcome us off our airplanes, thank you.

I don't remember doing much when I got home. I visited my friend Colin at the Veteran's Home in Chula Vista. I bought a new pair of running shoes and I generally just appreciated this pocket of time and space offset from the reality of Iraq. Our apartment was on the west side of the Highway 58 split and north of the east-west lay of Interstate 15 which connects Los Angeles with Las Vegas. It was like a wooded shadow glen, green with shade in the Barstow desert. I ran up and down my hill across Jasper Road, across Main Street, and across the railroad tracks. I would stack rocks on the first hill just to mark time. I even built a little handrail. I would run further south to the next hill and then the ridgeline where you eventually reach a fence overlooking the 15 on the L.A. side. There's an American flag that waves there. Whomever owns that tract of land changes it out on occasion. Also whomever owned that land eventually sold the part that had that hill; or, developed it a bit because it is gone now. Years later when visiting I drove by my old apartment and turned right to go under the rail overpass out onto Main Street and the hill was gone. The whole hill. I would have never thought that I wouldn't be able to return to that place and find my pile of rocks. Nope.

I flew out to Kuwait from Ontario and returned to Iraq after a sandstorm had delayed the helicopters – our preferred rides back to our units. No one wants to drive. Back on Kalsu I head back to my tent (we had real-estate here in between Iskan and Diyarah) and found my commander,

"Sir, how are you? How is Maxine," I asked?

My commander whisked me aside from a few of the other sergeants who were doing whatever and I just figured it couldn't be good,

"She got shot."

Maxine was growing and she was reaching maturity and not having a vet handy means that she was also growing wild, unvaccinated, and rabies was definitely a possibility. She had accompanied us on many patrols and was loved near and far in our sector but was becoming increasingly more aggressive. She bit a sergeant and she had to be put down after that. It's widely practiced in Iraq as dogs are unclean to Muslims and it is not out of character to put wild dogs down as they are aggressive, carry disease, and bring all bad things with them. My commander had taken it upon himself to let me know.

Really not a moment to spare from here on out though. It was the bottom of October. Battle X-Ray (our command net) called that afternoon with a sudden need to check out an IED on Route Cleveland nearest to Haswah at the Jackson turn. It was near dark by the time we got there and this meant we had to get closer than usual to look into a crater where it was reported to be. There are few things funnier than a bunch of Soldiers in a vehicle trying to edge up to see just over the rim of a hole that was the home of a former IED and could easily be used to plant a new one. Screaming and shouting "Forward" and then "BACK BACK BACK". It's a riot. There was no IED but that was my first day back with about 60 days to go.

A few days later was Halloween. Same place almost as the IED but just a little further past the canal that skirted the backside (the east side) of Haswah. The first farms after leaving the small city. A first lieutenant with the 155th Mississippi Rifles was operating with another MiTT element and had been blown to bits not a few minutes before. The Iraqi Soldier that had been standing next to him only lost a finger. The lieutenant was in so many pieces that the knowledge of the proximity of the two men and their entirely different outcomes to that IED was mind-boggeling. When we first got there the lieutenant had parked us near side back 300 meters. He kept us there and walked forward to make liaison and ascertain if and how we could help.

Another bright and sunny day. It was a nice day. It really was. Blue sky, the heat was there but we were most certainly okay in it by now. The green of the fields again. So green. Incredibly beautiful to be between these reeds and canals and various farms of the Mesopotamian Valley in spring and summer. The radio came back with our commander telling us not to come forward and his voice was distraught. Most of us were on at least our second tour. That is pretty much why we had these senior and trusted billets as trainer-leaders in combat. It just comes off odd and laughable really. After hearing the jeering of our reaction the spirit of Halloween, I made a ghost noise into the radio: Oooooooooh. That didn't go over too well.

The commander called me forward. When I got there I had to basically just hear him out. He was not happy but he was good with it enough to understand - and that was that in that moment. However, there was still the lieutenant in fifty pieces and his commander bent over picking him up and placing his remains on a poncho for dignified return and burial. Then there was the Iraqi that was standing next to him. His hand was bandaged now. All of this sort of just ran together, much like the narrative of combat does. The next moment my commander ordered me to look for the trigger men.

I called forward a few of the sergeants and walked off to search the area. I came upon a nearby farmhouse and there were two 12-year old boys: Both cross-eyed. I just stood there and marveled at something that held a unique possibility in the realm of coordinated attacks but still wasn't formed in my language yet. Just the fact that they were boys and both cross-eyed was too much for me to believe that they were any harm. They were the only men around. They were 12. My commander was still heated and he wanted me to detain them, but I just couldn't without opening up the ICOM and simply stating that they were cross-eyed. Unless they were somehow working in tandem to pick out a target, I wasn't too sure and so much so that I really had to suggest a, "No." He came around reasonably and let it go. It would surprise me if those two had killed the lieutenant, but it would impress me too. War is so nuts that this is very possible. However, I wasn't convinced. This is the general discipline and discretion practiced everyday by American Riflemen around the world. We're smart and caring professionals and with each new war – a living library of expertise in the art of war in the flesh. Whomever killed the man I will call Lieutenant Ski from here on out also made him famous.

There was an underground newspaper called The Dixie Blunder. This was meant to be a parody of The Dixie Thunder, which is the motto of the 155th "Mississippi Rifles" Infantry Regiment. It's a proud tradition which I guess reflects that of my Iraqis who were all from the same town. These men and women all had to basically go home and see each other when it was all over. However, some were not even from there like some of the officers who may have been fulfilling other operational requirements along their career path. I don't know if Lieutenant Ski was a Dixie Man but I know he had a sense of humor and was deeply critical of sub-standard performers who had fallen completely out of regulations but had to be given the same respect and dignity. I know this and we know this because in his personal effects was the remainder of his publishing operation. I don't have a copy but Lieutenant Ski was a Patriot. He obviously believed in what he was doing and really could not stand so many of his peers and counterparts falling apart out in the open and no-one whether they wanted to do anything about it or not – could actually do anything about it. You learn here that most of society is formed this way: You have a dedicated and enfranchised bunch and you have the remainder. The remainder is not good or bad in its outright self, but in an Army – the remainder is to be discarded as soon as counsel and remediation fail. There is a noble and dignified process for this. However, combat knows very little except life or death and not much between. Moving too quickly to stop a war machine for the riff-raff. There's as much drag as there is speed I guess. Good Soldiers get really upset with this though because being invested means ownership and it's all we have: Our discipline; our conduct at the very edge of civilized action. It has to be right or it's immoral because of so many reasons to include just being out of shape and not being able to pull one's own weight when there is no strength to spare between the hardiest. It's not Sparta, but also it is. There's plenty of redemption in an Army. Plenty of space to work out things if you need to. It's up to the Soldier.

We were split in two when we arrived: One half of us went to Mosul and one half of us to Northern Babylon. People were looking up and down the country for the author of The Dixie Blunder between both places. Officers were heated over this obviously. Any commander is going to squash that immediately, true or not. The commander is the law in combat. Any grievances are his or her responsibility to take up without delay. Having an insurgency within the unit is not optimal for maintaining good order. Lieutenant Ski died an honorable man on October 31st, 2005 in Haswah, Iraq as a result of an improvised-explosive device and as a Patriot as the author of "The Dixie Blunder" - which was the best he could do to signal to others that our professionalism, vigilance, and righteousness was to be addressed – even if it had to be done clandestinely.

Every year I celebrate him. He owns Halloween. He is the best scary story ever and I have nothing but love and admiration for him.

As autumn was setting in and the land started to cool, we would greet local officials and our new company commander would host them in Diyarah's largest room which had been made in the manner of our true hosts: Grand, Arabic, and plenty of simple refreshments like Chai and bread. High ceiling, elaborate rugs across the floor. Islamic geometry everywhere. Our new commander was a suave man with a keen understanding of being a gracious host and he would liken it to diplomacy by offering a Pepsi. Many of the senior leaders of our troop were very convinced that if Iraqis had a speak-easy system of establishments beyond the family rigor, that maybe their condition would better as networks grew more objectively from random encounters instead of rigorous family lines that have elasticity. Again, not really our place to say – only suggest and to set the example that we intend for mimic and development of tables in the future. A more peaceful land by way of these simple social constructs without long-term binds.

One late afternoon in November, a farmer came to our firebase and said he had found two artillery shells in his field and wanted us to take a look and see what we could do to get them out of there. I mean, you can't run a till too many times over that dirt before your time and probability run out on you. I took my section of sergeants and we went over to the field about a quarter mile north and to the right. I viewed the land. The farmer took me by the hand and led me carefully forward. I casually got eyes on both and went back to the trucks and called for EOD (Explsive Ordnance Disposal).

We cooked MREs and waited for EOD – which takes a long time usually because like I said in the beginning, the mode of war here is the bomb. These are not lightfighters like Afghanis. EOD was forever busy in Iraq and the queue for units waiting for their expertise and courage stacked up day in and day out. A lot of stress.

Surprisingly they showed up within the hour and when the sergeant got there he asked me where the shells were. I led him forward and as we got closer he started to get weary and I had to stop to understand but before I did I simply asked him how his day was going.

"Where are the markings," he asked?

Oh, ya some markers would have helped but I knew where they were and we can drop them now.

I said the same thing outloud to him.

He raced back to his truck and started calling squadron and it took me a minute to realize he was calling Battle X-Ray regarding me. It took a hot minute to reassure him that it was simply a matter of me being accountable for their location with a high degree of measure and that these rounds were probably from fire missions past and not in any way IEDs. I apologized for not marking everything and he rescinded. To this day, I still have objects from my marking systems in the Army catalogued in my mind: How they are constructed, the merits of these, and of course the sound utility and efficiency that any organization benefits from with highly-coordinated symbolic guides and libraries. From hobo-markings to warchalking to advanced syntax; to Greenwich Mean Time (symbol: clock). The things we all synchronize by from little guy to big guy and back. By now in the deployment though, my eyes and my personal presence on a patch of dirt was marker enough. It was but just not for him in the moment. Glad it all worked out. Enough on marking systems.

We had a false start prior to our actual date for withdrawing from our sector as a brigade from the 4th Infantry Division was set to start entering North Babil as we had done almost a year before. We were told to close operations with our Iraqi Company and that meant standing Captain Majid's company up for independent operations – his company to be OpCon (operationally-controlled) from here on out exclusively with the Iraqi Army. Captain Majid found us as we were headed off to make liaison with a Captain W inside the old hospital at Iskan. He was visibly frightened and for the first time, Thundercat 6 (our commander), dropped his role as mentor and became a fellow officer to Majid.

"You can't leave us," he said in English. "We will die."

Both me and the commander thought, Yes – probably.

However that wasn't what came out. We all three laughed in the main doorway. Imagine any sliding glass doors of the lobby of a hospital. Whooshing back and forth and sun shining through the glass in late day. There was no whoosh to our hospital doors. They were broken.

"You're going to be fine," we both said. We believed our training of them and their progress was on par. We were both particularly impressed how honest he was.

Thundercat 6 and I walked down to meet a Captain W. If I remember it had to do with some sidebar annex for this stand-down with the Iraqi Army and rejoining of main forces. We chatted about 45 minutes. Captain W took off with his convoy. The commander and I had some other business to attend to while we were at this end of the facility (The MiTT side I guess). Not 45 minutes later the radio came to life with the death of Captain W. He was just here. Now he wasn't. Just like that.

On one of the last meetings we had with Majid he was very much in his element as a commander: He had swagger. Bold Arabian swagger. He sat as an officer and a gentleman and reached across the table to say hi to me in front of his men as an equal, if only for a minute,

"Good evening, Arif (Comes out like A REEF, and was their term for Sergeant) Lombardy," said Captain Majid.

"Good evening, Sir," I replied.

Killer Cam and Thundercat 6 were always battling each other for the last word. Even on tactical nets. When the call came to leave and we were all lined up for our final run down Route Cleveland one December afternoon, I was recording Killer Cam give his final sentiments on everything here,

"All I gotta say is this place will not be missed. Well maybe a little bit; but - I'm not going to lose any sleep over it."

Just as I was about to cut the camera, Thundercat 6 squawked over the radio,

"Any Reaper Red Element this is Thundercat 6."

Cam just started laughing.

Like clockwork, Thundercat 6 got the last word at the last moment without even being co-located. I stopped recording and we made one final sprint down Route Cleveland. Like the wind.

On a December morning just before Christmas I grabbed my bags and was herded out to the same rocky helicopter pad I had landed at on a January night 12 months before. It was daytime. It was nice out. Mortars fell this time. A going-away gift from the pre-image of who would become ISIS. None of us even moved. They hit nearby and we watched and we laughed.

In the strangest and most cartoon way this story of Iraq could end, my wife picked me up at night, I popped the trunk, placed my bags inside, slammed the trunk down, and thought of my commander. Twelve months earlier I had been standing in the same parking space expecting to die this way. I was tired now. We drove through the desert where there are several dozen white crosses from all of the fatal accidents leading in and out of the National Training Center. We stopped at McDonald's at Barstow Station and returned home to our place on Jasper Drive.

The End